Walking
FOR
Health

 Wm. C. Brown Publishers

Walking
F O R
Health

Lon H. Seiger
Assistant Professor, Delta State University

James Hesson
Assistant Professor, Delta State University

Foreword by Charles F. Brock, Jr., M.D.

 Wm. C. Brown Publishers

Book Team

Editor *Edward E. Bartell*
Production Coordinator *Kay Driscoll*

Wm. C. Brown Publishers

President *G. Franklin Lewis*
Vice President, Publisher *George Wm. Bergquist*
Vice President, Publisher *Thomas E. Doran*
Vice President, Operations and Production *Beverly Kolz*
National Sales Manager *Virginia S. Moffat*
Advertising Manager *Ann M. Knepper*
Editor in Chief *Edward G. Jaffe*
Production Editorial Manager *Colleen A. Yonda*
Production Editorial Manager *Julie A. Kennedy*
Publishing Services Manager *Karen J. Slaght*
Manager of Visuals and Design *Faye M. Schilling*

Cover design by Jeanne Marie Regan

Printed in the United States of America by Wm. C. Brown Publishers, 2460 Kerper Boulevard, Dubuque, IA 52001

10 9 8 7 6 5 4 3 2 1

Dedication

This book is dedicated to everyone who has helped us learn.

Contents

Healthy Life-Style   139

14

Foreword

Medical research indicates that regular exercise performed at a moderate level of exertion can make a positive contribution to an individual's health. Exercise is especially beneficial for reducing the risk of cardiovascular disease and musculoskeletal conditions. For many, the emotional or psychological benefits of exercise are as important as the physical benefits. Most individuals report that they feel better once they begin a regular exercise program.

Walking is an attractive exercise alternative. It can be recommended for those who are healthy, and can be prescribed for many who are not. Because walking is a familiar activity, it is relatively easy for the patient to commit to a walking program.

Cardiovascular disease and obesity are major health problems in the United States. Walking is an excellent exercise for those who are overweight because it reduces body fat and develops the cardiovascular system. In addition, the risk of injury is lower since walking does not place as much stress on the bones and joints as some other popular activities.

WALKING FOR HEALTH is a valuable source of information for those who desire a safe and enjoyable exercise program.

Charles F. Brock, Jr., M.D.

Preface

This book has been developed to assist walkers of any age, sex, background, and skill level to acquire the knowledge, skills, and attitudes necessary for participation in a lifelong fitness walking program.

The material is presented in a style that is easy to understand for the beginning fitness walker; but intermediate and advanced levels of knowledge and skill can be achieved when the material is thoroughly mastered.

This is not intended to be a total fitness book. The focus of *Walking for Health* is on cardiovascular fitness and body composition—the components of health-related physical fitness that are of greatest concern in our society.

Activities are presented to provide meaningful learning experiences. Other special features include a walking test, three different walking programs, and guidelines for effective exercise.

The first chapter provides a brief overview of the popularity of walking. Chapter 2 outlines the benefits for fitness walkers. Chapter 3 describes clothing and equipment. Chapter 4 details safety considerations. Guidelines for warm-up, cool down, and flexibility are explained in chapter 5.

Chapter 6 describes the Rockport Fitness Walking Test. Chapter 7 illustrates fitness walking programs recommended by Rockport and the American Heart Association. In addition, guidelines for effective exercise are presented for those who prefer to develop their own fitness walking program. Fitness walking techniques are demonstrated in chapter 8.

The relationship of nutrition to good health and guidelines for eating a well-balanced diet are examined in chapter 9. Recommendations for weight loss in chapter 10, and the mental benefits described in chapter 11, are important to many walkers.

Chapter 12 provides motivational strategies for sticking with a fitness walking program. The beneficial effects of regular exercise during the aging process are described in chapter 13. Chapter 14 explains that fitness walking is only one part of a larger total health program.

We believe you will enjoy reading *Walking for Health* and find the information useful. Each day we make choices that either enhance or detract from our present health. Fitness walking is a positive choice that can make a significant contribution to a healthy life-style.

Acknowledgments

The authors wish to extend their appreciation to Clement Gee for the majority of the photography throughout the book; Bill Powell for his photographic contributions; Lori Atkins, Kippy Betts, Tammy Kelly, Laurita Koll, Maria Lee, Dixie Wright, Louise Kimmel, Ross Story, Penny Gong, Karen Williams, Clara Belle Wiley, and Roy Wiley for their time and patience as models; and Dr. Milton Wilder, Dr. Lisso Simmons, Dr. Frank McArthur, and Dr. Kent Wyatt for their support.

The Walking Boom

1

Over 77 million Americans have turned walking into the number one fitness activity in the United States. Experts predict that this number will soon increase to over 100 million.

Walking is one of the safest and most effective forms of exercise to improve health and develop physical fitness. Doctors are recommending walking as the best exercise for many Americans.

What Is Fitness Walking?

Fitness walking refers to the type of walking that produces health and fitness benefits. For walking to be considered fitness walking it must be done fast enough, long enough, and often enough to produce desirable health benefits. In addition, attention should be given to correct walking techniques.

More and more Americans are walking to improve their health and fitness.

More and more Americans are walking to improve their health and fitness.

Are There Organized Walking Events?

There are over 10,000 walking events held every year, and this number is increasing. In the striding events participants walk a six-mile course in paradelike fashion. Many of the events that used to be for runners only are now encouraging walkers to enter. There has also been an increase in the number of race walking events.

Are There Walking Clubs?

Walking clubs are being formed all over the country. Over 6,500 clubs are registered with *The Walking Magazine.* "The Walkers and Talkers" and "The Road Scholars" are the names of two clubs that have turned fitness walking into an enjoyable social event. Why not form a walking club in your area? It's a healthy way to spend time with friends.

What Is Mall Walking?

At many indoor shopping malls throughout the United States, walkers are allowed to exercise before the stores open. This has provided many walkers with a comfortable and dependable place to exercise all year. Mall walking offers the additional attractions of personal safety and group participation.

A walking event sponsored by the American Cancer Society.

Mall walking has become popular as a safe, climate-controlled fitness activity.

Are There Special Shoes for Fitness Walking?

The shoe industry provides further evidence of the growing popularity of fitness walking. A few years ago it was difficult to find a good pair of walking shoes, but now there are over forty companies making them. Some companies are taking the design features of their fitness walking shoes and including them in their dress shoes. It is now possible to wear comfortable shoes all day, not just when you exercise.

Where Can I Obtain Fitness Walking Information?

In recent years there has been an increase in the amount of fitness walking information that is available. This information has appeared in magazines, books, and brochures, as well as on television, radio, and video and audio cassettes.

Is Fitness Walking an Ideal Exercise?

In an age of high-tech exercise machines, why has there been all of this interest in a form of exercise as old as the human race? There may be as many reasons for this interest as there are fitness walkers. However, when all the reasons are considered, people are interested in fitness walking because it is an enjoyable way to improve their health.

Fitness walking can be an escape from the high-tech life-style. There are no machines, videos, or expensive club memberships. No one is excluded from fitness walking because of age, body type, or skill level. It can be done almost anywhere and at almost any time.

Fitness walking is a versatile exercise. It can be started on a small scale and increased as conditioning improves. The techniques are not difficult to learn, and there are several variations of walking to choose from: strolling, everyday walking, hiking, backpacking, snowshoeing, stairwalking, brisk walking, and race walking. You can probably think of other variations. These variations allow you to find the best workout for your age, interest, and fitness level.

For the reasons mentioned above, and many others, health professionals are recommending fitness walking as an excellent form of exercise for all ages.

Can Walking Improve Physical Fitness?

For years it was thought that walking would not provide enough exercise to produce any cardiovascular benefit. Scientific research has proven that fitness walkers are able to reach the training heart rates necessary to produce an improvement in cardiovascular fitness.

When using correct walking techniques and accelerated arm and leg movements fitness walking involves most of the muscles in your body. Brisk walking produces an increased oxygen demand. This increased demand for oxygen makes your circulatory and respiratory systems work harder than usual, which improves the functioning of your heart and lungs.

Is Walking Slow and Boring?

Walking can be fast and interesting. Walking speeds may vary from a slow shuffle of less than one mile per hour to race walking at speeds in excess of ten miles per hour. World-class race walkers can walk sub-six-minute miles, and maintain that speed for more than twelve miles. Most people could not run even one sub-six-minute mile, much less maintain that speed for twelve miles.

Fitness walkers generally walk a mile in about twelve to seventeen minutes. Using proper form, with accelerated arm and leg swings, speed can be dramatically increased.

With a positive attitude walking is not boring. There are many interesting things you can do while you walk. Some ideas include listening to a tape player to learn something new, listening to your favorite music, listening to the news, talking with friends, releasing stress, solving personal problems, exploring new areas, appreciating nature, praying, and meditating.

Is Walking Only for the Old and Injured?

It is true that fitness walking is an excellent exercise for older people, for cardiac patients, and for those who have been injured. However, walking is not limited to those people. Fitness walking is a safe and effective form of exercise that is also being used by young, healthy individuals who want to become more fit.

Who Is Robert Sweetgall?

Some of the increased awareness of and interest in fitness walking may be traced to Robert Sweetgall. Within one year, Robert lost several family members to heart disease, the leading cause of death in the United States. The losses encouraged him to change his life and communicate to Americans the importance of fitness.

After a year of training and planning, Robert set out to complete the "50/50: Walk for the Health of It." His mission was to walk through all fifty states in fifty weeks to demonstrate and communicate the value of fitness walking for cardiovascular health. His walk across America reached millions of people with the message that fitness walking is an exercise almost anyone can do to keep healthy.

Robert Sweetgall, who walked across America to promote fitness walking.

The United States is experiencing a walking boom. You have probably noticed the increased number of people in your community who are walking to improve their health and fitness. Why not choose to do something positive about your own health and fitness? Join the fitness walking movement.

Activity 1a

The purpose of this activity is to observe the popularity of fitness walking.

Early in the morning, before most people go to work, or in the evening, after most people get home from work, see how many people you can find walking for exercise. Look in your neighborhood, local parks, outdoor tracks, and other likely places.

Count the number of people you see walking for exercise during a thirty-minute time period.

Benefits of Fitness Walking

2

Why Exercise?

Of the ten leading causes of death in the United States, nine are related to life-style (see table 2.1). One of these harmful life-style behaviors is sedentary living. If you have a sedentary life-style there will be a gradual decline in your body's ability to function. If this deterioration is allowed to continue, eventually one of your organ systems will not be able to perform its life-sustaining function. If this occurs you will experience a life-threatening illness, or death.

Long before death, however, there may be years of "not feeling very good." Nothing definite, no specific symptoms, just an overall feeling that life is difficult and not enjoyable and that it is about all you can do to get through another day. These are feelings that are frequently expressed by people who are in poor physical condition.

The good news is that a moderate amount of exercise on a regular basis will improve the functioning of your body. Exercise can help you look better, feel better, and enjoy life. It is difficult to explain how good life can be when you are in excellent health and excellent physical condition. Wouldn't you like to look great, feel great, and enjoy life?

Table 2.1   The Ten Leading Causes of Death in the United States for All Ages.

Rank	Cause
1	Heart Disease
2	Cancer
3	Stroke
4	Accidents
5	Chronic Lung Disease
6	Pneumonia and Influenza
7	Diabetes
8	Suicide
9	Cirrhosis of the Liver
10	Atherosclerosis

Source: National Center for Health Statistics, United States Department of Health and Human Services.

Why Aerobic Exercise?

You are an aerobic organism. The term *aerobic* (a-rōw'-bik) refers to life forms that require oxygen. In recent years it has also been used to identify exercises that require you to use large amounts of oxygen. You could live weeks without eating, days without water, but only about five to ten minutes without oxygen. How well your body operates depend on your ability to get oxygen to every living cell.

Oxygen is brought into your body with the air you breathe into your lungs. Approximately one-fifth of normal unpolluted air is oxygen. Some of the oxygen that has entered your lungs is transferred into your blood. Your heart then pumps the oxygenated blood to all of your cells.

Any life-style behavior that reduces the functioning of your respiratory or circulatory systems also reduces your ability to get life-sustaining oxygen to your cells. Sedentary living reduces your ability to deliver oxygen to all parts of your body. This decline in oxygen delivery could be considered a slow form of suffocation, and results in "not feeling very good." If this deterioration continues, eventually you will only be able to take in enough oxygen to sustain your life in a resting state. This does not leave any room for adjustment to an increased demand, such as a physical or emotional emergency.

A poorly conditioned person may experience a sudden demand for increased oxygen delivery. Because their body is not capable of delivering more oxygen to the heart muscle, which is now working harder than usual, some of the oxygen-starved heart muscle tissue may die. The affected cardiac muscle tissue can no longer contract. Therefore the heart may not be able to continue to pump oxygenated blood to any of the other living cells of the body. This is a simplified explanation of one type of heart attack. Of course, without a continuous supply of life-sustaining oxygen the other cells of the body cannot survive either.

Because humans are aerobic organisms, exercises that improve the ability to obtain and use oxygen are best. These aerobic exercises stimulate development of the oxygen delivery system and typically use large muscle groups in a rhythmic and continuous manner. Listed in table 2.2 are some of the benefits of aerobic exercise.

Table 2.2   Benefits of Aerobic Exercise

The following benefits have been reported as a result of a moderate amount of aerobic exercise performed on a regular basis. While all of these benefits are still under investigation, some have been studied more thoroughly than others. Biological adaptation to exercise is a gradual process that requires consistent and long-term participation.

Heart

—Increased strength of the heart muscle

—Increased stroke volume

—Increased cardiac output

—Increased heart volume

—Decreased resting heart rate

—Decreased exercise heart rate at a standard work load

Table 2.2   Benefits of Aerobic Exercise (continued)

Heart

—Decreased risk of cardiovascular disease

—Decreased risk of heart attack

—Decreased severity of heart attack if one does occur

—Increased chance of surviving a heart attack if one does occur

Blood

—Increased blood flow

—Increased total blood volume

—Increased number of red blood cells

—Increased oxygen-carrying capacity of the blood

—Increased high-density lipoproteins

—Increased ability to extract oxygen from the blood

—Decreased harmful blood fats

—Decreased total cholesterol

Blood Vessels

—Increased size of capillaries

—Increased number of open capillaries

—Increased peripheral circulation

—Increased coronary circulation

—Decreased resting blood pressure for some individuals

—Decreased risk of atherosclerosis

Lungs

—Increased minute volume of air

—Increased rate of breathing during exercise

—Increased volume per breath during exercise

Body Fat

—Decreased total body fat

—Decreased percent body fat

—Maintain healthy body fat level

—Decreased appetite if exercise is performed just before a meal

—Decreased total body weight

Muscle

—Increased lean body weight

—Increased muscle tissue

—Increased muscle strength

—Increased muscle endurance

Bone

—Increased bone density

—Increased bone strength

—Increased joint strength

—Decreased risk of osteoporosis

Table 2.2   Benefits of Aerobic Exercise (continued)

Connective Tissue
—Increased tendon strength
—Increased ligament strength
—Increased joint strength

Endurance
—Increased work efficiency
—Increased sports performance
—Increased ability to use oxygen
—Increased physical ability to meet emergency situations
—Increased recovery after hard work
—Increased cardiovascular endurance
—Increased functioning of oxygen-supply organ systems

Resistance to Disease
—Increased resistance to disease
—Increased health

Appearance
—Improved appearance
—Improved posture
—Decreased waistline

Stress
—Decreased emotional stress

Mental
—Increased self-concept
—Increased positive attitude
—Increased self-confidence
—Increased self-discipline
—Increased positive feeling
—Increased independence for many older citizens
—Decreased depression
—Increased soundness of sleep
—Decreased mental tension
—Increased social interaction with healthy people
—Increased resistance to fatigue
—Increased feeling of success
—Increased enjoyment of leisure time
—Increased enjoyment of work
—Increased quality of life
—Increased sense of well-being

Six major aerobic activities: (a) walking, (b) swimming, (c) aerobic dancing, (d) water aerobics, (e) bicycling, and (f) jogging.

Walking is a life-long exercise.

Why Fitness Walking?

Fitness walking is an excellent aerobic exercise for many reasons.

Lifelong Exercise

To get the greatest benefit from exercise it must be consistent and lifelong, twelve months a year, every year, not seasonal.

Walking is the preferred exercise of many adults because it can be done almost anywhere and almost anytime. Unlike some sports, walking is an exercise you can perform for the rest of your life.

Everyone Can Participate

Walking has few restrictions. Almost everyone can participate in fitness walking. No special sports skills are necessary in order to achieve a beneficial amount of exercise.

If you happen to be overweight, walking is ideal because it puts less strain on your bones and joints than some of the other aerobic activities.

All body types can participate in fitness walking.

Posture

Fitness walking promotes good posture by strengthening many of your muscles. Good posture allows you to function more effectively, expending a minimum amount of energy. With good posture there is less strain on your muscles, tendons, ligaments, and joints. Good posture also conveys alertness, confidence, and attractiveness.

Cardiac Rehabilitation

Walking is the primary exercise for many cardiac rehabilitation programs. It is a good exercise for those recovering from heart attacks because walking is an exercise that they are familiar with, are not afraid of, can continue for the rest of their life, can easily monitor, can start at a low level, and can progressively increase.

Walking gets heart attack victims on their feet again. It helps them regain some control of their lives and feel optimistic about the future.

Rehabilitation of Injuries

Walking can be an excellent exercise to help recover from injuries, especially leg injuries. When muscles are not used they atrophy (decrease in size and strength). Walking can be an important exercise in the recovery process because it helps to rebuild muscle tissue.

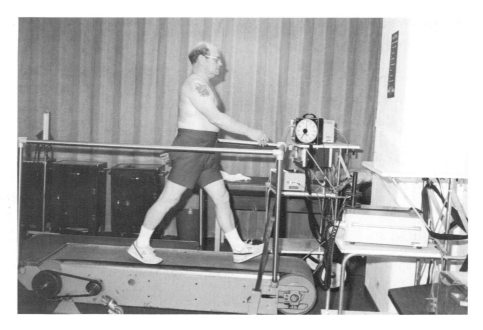

Walking is an ideal exercise for cardiac rehabilitation patients.

An injured football player walks to aid the recovery process.

Safe and Natural Exercise

Many former joggers have changed to fitness walking. The force of landing on each foot during walking is about 1 to 1½ times your body weight. The force of landing on each foot during jogging is about 3½ to 4 times your body weight. Therefore, joint and muscle injuries are less likely to occur with a walking program.

Walking produces balanced leg muscle development and is one of the most natural exercises for the human body. Your body was designed for movement, not inactivity.

Fitness Walking Is Inexpensive

Fitness walking does not require expensive facilities, equipment, or membership. Of course, as fitness walking continues its rapid growth in popularity, creative people will develop innovative products, facilities, clothing, equipment, and memberships that will find a market. If you enjoy these new products and services, have a desire for them, and can afford them, that's fine—just remember that they are not necessary for you to gain the benefits from fitness walking.

Fitness Walking Can Help You Get Fit for Sports

You can start slowly with fitness walking and gradually build to a high level of fitness. For people who have not been exercising, walking is recommended as a starter program to prepare for participation in sports.

Easier to Stick With

The dropout rate for fitness walking is lower than it is for other exercise programs. Walking is convenient and accessible. It can be used as a form of transportation. Walking can be combined with other enjoyable activities such as sightseeing and carrying on a conversation. Because walking is more enjoyable than some of the other fitness activities, you are more likely to stick with your exercise program.

Social Activity

Walking is an excellent family and group activity. It can be a social activity and a fitness activity at the same time. Joggers often have difficulty maintaining a conversation while they exercise. Walkers are more likely to maintain a conversation due to the lower intensity and longer duration of many walking programs.

Walking provides an excellent opportunity for family members and friends to spend regular time together. It provides a time to discuss personal and family needs, wants, goals, and dreams.

Instead of going out for dinner, dessert, or a drink, why not go out for a walk together?

Walking is a convenient and enjoyable method of transportation.

Family and friends can enjoy walking together.

Weight Loss

Fitness walking is an excellent way to lose weight. Because many people are interested in losing excess body fat, an entire chapter is devoted to this important benefit of fitness walking.

Walking gives you the opportunity to enjoy nature.

Appreciating the Outdoors

One of the advantages of walking is that it provides an opportunity to get outdoors. Many people in the United States spend the majority of their time indoors. Fitness walking is a good way to explore your surroundings and discover the beauty around you. Hiking and backpacking are popular forms of walking.

Exercise During Pregnancy

Walking is one of the safest and best exercises during pregnancy. What many women do when they find out they are pregnant is stop all physical activity and become totally deconditioned for the most demanding physical activity of their lives. When they do finally give birth, they are often in their weakest and poorest physical condition as a result of nine months of deconditioning. Adequate exercise and good nutrition bring many benefits to the developing child as well as the mother.

Fitness walking is a good exercise for pregnant women because it is a low impact activity. Also, the intensity level can be easily monitored and adjusted to the fairly rapid biological changes that occur during pregnancy.

Walking is an excellent exercise during pregnancy.

Walking is an excellent exercise after pregnancy.

Walking can fit into anyone's daily routine.

Exercise After Pregnancy

Walking is an excellent exercise after pregnancy. You can start slowly and progress gradually as your fitness level improves. You can begin immediately to lose excess body fat that may have been gained during pregnancy and begin to get your figure back. At the same time you will be building cardiovascular endurance, which you will definitely need as a mother.

Walking is not only a good exercise, it is also good for stress management. It provides an opportunity to get out of the house and enjoy being outdoors. You can take your new baby along in a stroller, the stimulation of new surroundings is good for young children. Or you can leave the new baby with Dad for thirty to sixty minutes while you take an exercise break.

Fits In with Your Daily Routine

You may choose to walk at a time that best fits your schedule. Some people prefer to walk early in the morning to start the day. Others prefer to walk late at night at the end of their day. Still others choose to walk at noon or during breaks. These are only a few of the ways people fit walking into their daily routine.

Activity 2a

The purpose of this activity is to determine the specific reasons for your participation in a fitness walking program.

On a blank sheet of paper, list the benefits you would like to receive from your fitness walking program. Don't evaluate them at this time, just list them as quickly as you can think of them. When you can't think of any more, go back and place a check next to the top three benefits you hope to achieve. Of those three, which one is the most important to you? Why?

Clothing and Equipment

3

One of the advantages of fitness walking is that you don't need to spend a lot of money on special clothing and equipment. Some activities, such as skiing and scuba diving, require expensive equipment that might only be used once or twice a year. Most fitness walking clothing and equipment is relatively inexpensive and can be used every day.

The most important piece of clothing or equipment you can buy for fitness walking is a good pair of walking shoes.

Walking Shoes

Approximately 87 percent of all Americans have suffered from foot problems, many of which are caused by wearing shoes that do not fit properly, or shoes that are worn out. When shopping for shoes, it is wise to spend a little extra time and money to get good quality and a proper fit. You can not buy a new pair of feet.

When shopping for fitness walking shoes be sure to allow enough time. Do not try to do it in five minutes. Be a good comparison shopper. Try on at least three different brands and as many styles as possible. Even if a shoe is ranked as the best, or most popular, it may not fit you as comfortably as another brand or model.

Walking shoes should feel comfortable when you first try them on. There is very little "break in" necessary for good quality walking shoes. Be wary of the salesperson who tells you an uncomfortable pair of walking shoes will feel fine after you break them in.

When you try on walking shoes, test them on a hard surface instead of the padded carpet commonly found in shoe stores. This will help you determine the amount of cushion and comfort the shoes provide.

Outer Sole

The outer sole is the material on the bottom of a shoe. It should be made from a durable material. A good walking shoe has a rocker shaped sole, which helps your foot rock forward from heel to toe.

Walking shoes have a tread design for traction, but it is not as deep as commonly found on running shoes.

Some people experience eversion when they walk or run. Eversion is the anatomical term for a foot movement in which the bottom of the foot turns outward. Commercially, the term pronation is being used instead of eversion to describe this foot movement and has gained popular acceptance. *Pronation* is actually an anatomical term describing a forearm movement.

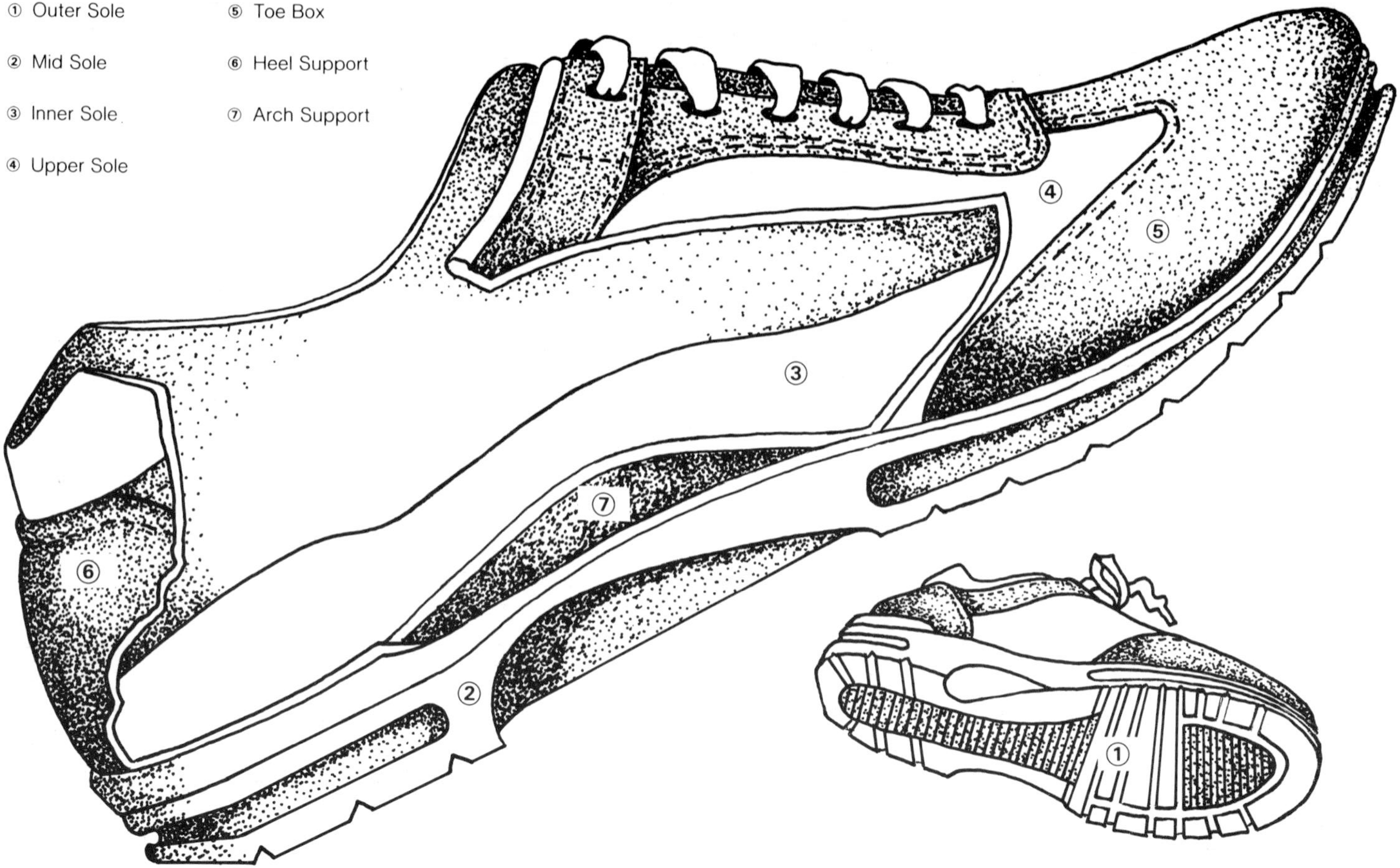

Important components of a high-quality walking shoe.

① Outer Sole   ⑤ Toe Box

② Mid Sole   ⑥ Heel Support

③ Inner Sole   ⑦ Arch Support

④ Upper Sole

A shoe with antipronation construction is designed to keep the sole of your foot from turning too far outward. If excessive pronation occurs with every step you take, extensive jogging or walking could eventually result in injury. Therefore, some of the better running and walking shoes have antipronation construction for those who need the extra support.

Midsole

The midsole is a cushioning layer between the outer and inner sole. Because the primary purpose of the midsole is to absorb shock, it can be made from a variety of materials and can be designed in many different ways.

There is no exact way for most people to determine when the midsole has lost its ability to absorb shock. The outer sole and upper part of the shoe may look fine, but if the midsole has lost its resiliency, it is time to get a new pair of walking shoes.

Inner Sole

The inner sole makes direct contact with your foot. This sole should include an arch support and a heel cup. Some shoes have an arch support that can be added to or removed from the inner sole. The inner sole may also provide additional air or gel cushioning.

The inner sole can be removed from many high quality walking shoes. One advantage of this is to let the inner sole air out after a workout. A second advantage is that it can be replaced if it wears out. A third advantage is that a podiatrist or an orthopedic doctor can make an inner sole that is just right for your foot.

Upper Shoe

The upper shoe is often made of leather because it is a durable material that is supple. The toe box portion of the shoe should be wide enough that the front part of your foot can spread out. This will allow you to push off with all of your toes.

The heel of the upper shoe should include a stiff material to provide support and hold your foot in position. Good walking shoes have a notch at the top of the heel support to minimize irritation of the Achilles tendon.

Some walking shoes have reflective material, as a safety measure, for those who walk in the dark.

Size and Comfort

One of your feet may be longer than the other. Try on both shoes. Purchase shoes that are comfortable for the longest foot. You may need to wear an extra sock on the smaller foot if there is a big difference.

It is a good idea to try shoes on before you buy them. You may find that different brands of shoes fit differently, even if the size marked on the shoes is the same. Also, the size of your feet may change.

If you choose to buy your walking shoes through a mail order company, make sure they have a return policy.

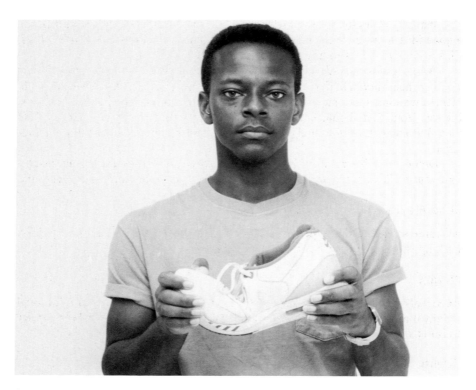

A good walking shoe is flexible.

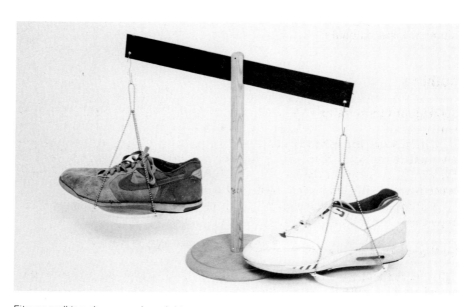

Fitness walking shoes vary in weight.

Walking shoes do not require much of a break-in period. However, it is still a good idea to alternate your old shoes with your new shoes for a couple weeks. This allows your feet to gradually adjust to the change.

Walking shoes should fit comfortably, not too tight or too loose. Your fitness walking shoes should fit like a glove. They need to be long enough and wide enough. Fitness walking shoes should be at least one-fourth of an inch longer than your big toe. Your feet should not feel squeezed into a shoe that is too narrow. You may find some variation in the size of sports shoes depending on the manufacturer.

Do not sacrifice comfort for name brand, style, or sale price. It is important that your walking shoes be comfortable. Your feet should not hurt when you walk.

Shoe Flexibility

All three soles and the upper shoe should bend at the ball of your foot. A good walking shoe should not be stiff at this point.

Weight

Race walking shoes are lighter than training shoes. A few ounces of additional weight may make a difference in a race. However, most fitness walkers prefer training shoes that are more durable.

Quality

Look carefully at walking shoes. Is the shoe made from quality materials? Is the shoe put together well? Is the stitching done carefully? Is the upper shoe securely fastened to the midsole?

Fitness walking shoes are an investment in your health. Make a good investment. Insist on quality.

Clothing

Clothing for fitness walking should be light weight and allow freedom of movement.

Cotton socks are excellent for absorbing moisture. For extra comfort you may want to put on an extra pair of socks. Another option is to buy socks that have extra cushioning in the heel and forefoot area. This extra cushioning may reduce friction and help prevent blisters.

A sports bra for women and an athletic supporter for men will provide firm support and make fitness walking more comfortable.

Hot Weather Clothing

Light-colored and loose-fitting clothing are cooler during hot weather. Light-colored clothing reflects some of the suns rays and loose-fitting clothing allows air to circulate next to your skin. Both of these keep you cooler on a hot day.

(a)

(b)

(a) Hot and (b) cold weather clothing suitable for fitness walking.

Walking shorts should allow free and easy movement. Lightweight shorts with built-in briefs add support with little increase in bulk. Shorts that are made of thick material might have a bulky inseam that could rub on the inside of your thighs.

Another advantage of lightweight shorts is that they dry quickly. It is possible to rinse them out after each workout and have them clean and dry for the next day.

Shirts that are loose fitting and are made of natural fabrics, such as cotton, absorb perspiration and allow air next to your skin.

A good hot-weather walking hat should have a raised crown with vents to allow air to circulate between the top of the hat and your head. In sunny weather the brim of the hat should protect your eyes and forehead from the harmful rays of the sun. On hot, sunny days a hat helps prevent headaches and fatigue.

Cold Weather Clothing

For fitness walking in cold weather dress in layers of clothing. This will allow you to remove layers to regulate your body temperature as you walk. Keeping warm while exercising in cold weather is not as much of a problem as you might think. Approximately 75 percent of the energy released during muscle contraction is in the form of heat energy. Therefore, your muscles produce a lot of heat during exercise. You can use your layers of clothing to control how much heat you want next to your skin.

The first layer of clothing should be a material that will keep you warm and dry. It should draw moisture away from your skin because it is difficult to stay warm if you are wet. This layer should be a loose-weave fabric with air spaces that can hold warm air next to your skin.

The next layer on your upper body might be a long sleeved T-shirt or a turtleneck. On top of that add a wool pullover or a sweatshirt.

The top layer could be a cotton sweat suit or a synthetic fabric depending on the weather. If the weather is wet, the outer layer should be waterproof. If the weather is cold and windy, the outer layer should serve as a windbreaker.

Warm-up suits with air vents enhance evaporation. This reduces the moisture content inside the suit. These warm-up suits hold most of the heat in while allowing the moisture to escape.

A knit hat is recommended for cold weather. Wool is a popular material for warm knit hats. A hat or hood helps to hold in body heat. As much as two-thirds of your body heat can be lost from your head if it is not covered.

Gloves or mittens should be worn during fitness walking because the fingers are especially vulnerable to the cold. A woven material allows perspiration to be drawn away from your skin while a solid synthetic material allows perspiration to accumulate inside. Natural fabrics, such as cotton or wool, work well.

Body Suits

Body suits are available that are made of lycra or lycra blend material. They conform to the shape of your body but do not restrict your movement.

Sauna Suits

Rubber suits or sauna suits are dangerous and should not be worn. These suits are made of nonporous material. This means that air and moisture can not pass through. Sauna suits have elastic at the neck, wrist, waist, and ankle. During exercise the air between the suit and your skin becomes hot and humid. It is possible to experience extreme heat and humidity inside the sauna suit even on a comfortable day. Heat cramps, heat exhaustion, and heat stroke can occur.

Some people wear sauna suits during exercise so they will sweat more. They believe it is possible to sweat off body fat. Heavy sweating may result in a rapid but temporary weight loss. However, the pounds lost are due to a fluid loss, not a fat loss. The fluid and the weight are quickly regained with any food or liquid intake. This is an unhealthy and ineffective way to attempt to lose weight. A healthy way to lose weight and body fat is to use more calories than you take in.

Bodysuits.

A hazardous sauna suit.

Equipment

Fitness walking equipment can make walking safer and more enjoyable.

Sunglasses

Sunglasses are important to protect your eyes from the harmful direct rays of the sun and from reflected glare. The best sunglasses to use are the ones that provide UV (ultraviolet) protection. As a fitness walker it is possible to experience dizziness and temporary vision impairment if your eyes are not shielded from direct sunlight.

Reflective Material

Many people walk when it is dark. This is especially true during the winter months when the daylight hours are short. Reflective tape can be put on your walking clothes and shoes. Reflective vests are also available. If you decide not to use reflective material, at least wear light colored clothing that can be seen more easily in the dark.

Pulsemeter

A pulsemeter allows you to monitor your heart rate while you are walking. You need to reach a prescribed exercise heart rate to receive an adequate training

Fitness walking equipment.

effect. A pulsemeter can inform you when you have reached your exercise heart rate. It provides feedback that can be used to stay at the correct exercise heart rate for the duration of your walk.

Pedometer

A pedometer is a device that measures how far you walk. This is usually done by counting the number of steps you take. On some models you need to preset your approximate stride length.

Backpack

Backpacks are useful for one-day hikes and weekend trips. In your backpack you can carry first aid items, a change of socks, and extra layers of clothing. Waist packs are also available.

Hand Weights

Hand weights may be carried during fitness walking to increase your muscular effort, energy expenditure, oxygen demand, and heart rate. Beginners should not carry weights. The additional exercise load could be harmful for the unconditioned beginner. Hand weights are recommended for intermediate or advanced fitness walkers only.

Quality clothing and equipment can increase your fitness walking enjoyment.

Safety

4

Fitness walking has many benefits. However, as with any activity that involves human movement, care must be taken to avoid injury. Knowing some of the possible dangers in advance will enable you to walk safely.

Medical Clearance

You should get medical clearance from your physician before starting a fitness walking program.

Listen to Your Body

Each year, thousands of enthusiastic people, dedicated to new fitness goals, exercise too much the first day. This results in unnecessary pain and injury. When you begin an exercise program, start slowly.

The beneficial changes that occur in the human body, as a result of an exercise program, are best obtained if you start and progress slowly.

Activity 4a

The purpose of this activity is to help you determine if you are medically ready to participate in a fitness walking program. Answer each of the following questions:

1. Are you over thirty-five years of age?
2. Do you have any type of cardiovascular disease?
3. Do you have high blood pressure?
4. Do you ever experience chest pain?
5. Do you ever experience breathlessness?
6. Do you have any bone or joint problems?
7. Do you ever feel faint or dizzy?
8. Are you a smoker?
9. Have you been inactive for the last two years?
10. Do you have a weight problem?
11. Do you have any medical condition that could be a problem if you started walking?

If you responded with a yes to any of the questions, or if you have any doubt about your health, get medical clearance from your physician before starting a fitness walking program.

It is common to experience some mild muscle soreness a day or two after beginning a new exercise program. However, two of the best methods of relieving mild muscle soreness are static stretch and aerobic exercise. These are both included in your fitness walking workouts. After a few workouts your muscles will adapt to the new activity and the muscle soreness will go away.

If you progress slowly into your new exercise program, you should not experience any extreme pain. Pain is generally an indication of injury. If you do experience extreme pain, you should stop exercising and seek medical attention. Learn to listen to your body for feedback about the effects of your fitness walking program.

Walking During Extreme Weather Conditions

One excuse many people use for not exercising on a regular basis is the weather. Fitness walking can be done in a wide range of weather conditions. There are some dangers of exercising in extreme weather conditions, but if you know the dangers and take precautions, the weather should rarely be an excuse for not exercising.

Hot Weather Walking

The dangers of exercising in hot weather should be taken seriously. A loss of body fluid can impair performance. An excessive loss of body fluid may lead to heat cramps, heat exhaustion, and heat stroke. Those who are poorly conditioned, overfat, older, and not acclimatized to exercise in the heat have a higher risk. People who have previously suffered from heat disorders should be especially careful.

To reduce the risk of heat disorders, drink plenty of water about thirty minutes before walking. Continue to drink small amounts of water frequently during your workout. After exercising drink as much water as you want. Some studies have indicated that there is no such thing as drinking too much water. While there are many sports drinks on the market, plain water is hard to beat as a replacement fluid. Besides being absorbed quickly, it is generally the most available and least expensive fluid.

Other hot weather precautions include wearing light-colored, loose-fitting clothing, walking during the coolest times of the day, reducing exercise intensity, and reducing exercise duration. Remember, the purpose of exercise is to improve your health, not to endanger it.

Cold Weather Walking

Dehydration can be a problem when exercising during cold weather. Your body loses fluids more quickly than you realize. Perspiration is quickly evaporated when the weather is cold and dry. Even though you are not thirsty, drink plenty of water. It is also a good idea to avoid diuretic liquids, such as coffee and tea, which cause more frequent urination.

Frostbite is a cold weather danger, but with proper precautions it can be avoided. With freezing temperatures and windy conditions frostbite can occur within minutes on your hands, nose, ears, and toes. These are the most vulnerable parts of your body. Be sure that these areas are covered with clothing during extremely cold weather. If you are walking during cold weather and notice any tissue that is numb, or turning hard and white, take immediate action. Get indoors where the air temperature is warmer, and soak the tissue in warm water. Do not use hot water because tissue damage may occur.

Hypothermia is the term for low body temperature. For survival, the temperature inside your body must remain fairly constant at all times. Prolonged exposure to the cold, accompanied by excessive loss of body heat, can lead to a life-threatening condition in which your core body temperature drops to a dangerous level. The symptoms of hypothermia include disorientation, sluggishness, slurred speech, and a stumbling gait. Be sure you dress warm enough to maintain your core body temperature when walking during cold weather.

People with high blood pressure need to dress especially warm because shivering elevates blood pressure. Angina (chest pain) can also be a result of exposure to the cold. If you have angina, and the air temperature is low, wear a scarf that covers your mouth and nose. If you have any kind of cardiovascular disease, it is recommended that you walk indoors when the outdoor temperature drops below 20° F. Mall walking has become popular, especially in colder climates.

Because cold weather is often accompanied by snow and ice, the danger of slipping and falling is increased. It is a good idea to walk where other people will be around to help in case you happen to fall.

There is a myth that being in the cold will cause you to catch a cold. It is really airborne viruses from others that are the primary cause of the common cold. These are most frequently found indoors, in warm recirculated air, where we spend more time when the outside air temperature is low. Being in cold air can dry out the mucous membranes of your mouth and nose, which may make it easier for viruses to penetrate when you go indoors. Therefore, fitness walking during cold weather should not cause you to catch a cold as long as you enter a relatively virus-free environment when you go indoors.

When exercising in cold weather it is important to control the amount of heat lost from your body. In addition to dressing in layers of clothing, it is also important to cover your head and hands. As much as 70 percent of your body heat can be lost from your head and hands during cold weather if they are not covered.

As long as you are healthy and dress warmly, cold weather should not be a reason to miss your fitness walking workout.

Wet Weather Walking

Many beginning exercisers use wet weather as an excuse to skip their exercise session that day. Does this make sense? Human skin is amazingly waterproof. Besides these same people usually take a shower after exercise anyway, and get completely wet in the process. A large number of experienced fitness walkers and joggers enjoy a workout while it is raining or snowing. Remember how much fun it was to play in the rain when you were a child?

Rain is no barrier to fitness walking unless it's accompanied by lightning.

If you wish to try to stay dry while walking in the rain there are waterproof exercise suits available. Of course, if you walk vigorously, and produce a lot of perspiration, it will not evaporate on a rainy day anyway, because the air is already completely saturated with moisture. Therefore, you will be wet from perspiration instead of rain. Some of these water-resistant materials are expensive, but the cost is well worth it if a rain suit will help you stick with your walking program.

Walking in the rain or snow should not be harmful if you take a warm bath or shower, dry off, and put on warm dry clothing soon after you finish.

While the rain should not hurt you, lightning certainly could. It is one thing to walk in a nice soft rain shower and quite another to walk during a violent thunderstorm. If there is lightning outdoors find a way to exercise indoors for that day.

Drugs

There is no place in a health improvement program, such as fitness walking, for the use of recreational drugs.

If you are required to take prescription drugs for your health, consult with your physician before starting an exercise program. Exercise may alter the effects of the medicine.

Look directly into the driver's eyes before walking in front of a car.

Cars

When a car comes near you, look directly into the driver's eyes to determine if the driver has seen you. If you suspect that the driver has not seen you it is always best to move out of the way. If a walker has a collision with an automobile, it does not matter much who was right and who was wrong, the walker will be the big loser. Walk on the side of the road facing the oncoming traffic and walk defensively. Make it almost impossible for a car to hit you.

Bicycles

Bicycles are supposed to be ridden on the side of the road and in the same direction as the motor vehicle traffic. Bicycle riders are supposed to obey all traffic laws. However, if you find yourself on a collision course with a bicycle, it is generally easier for you to move out of the way than it is for the person on the bicycle. Walk defensively. Don't allow a bicycle to hit you.

Give bicyclists the right of way.

Dogs

No dog should have the right to decide where or when you can walk on public property. There are no guarantees, you have to make your own decision about what to do if a dog comes at you. However here are some ideas that have worked for others and may work for you.

If a dog comes at you do not run away. You cannot run faster than a dog, so it encourages the dog to continue the chase. You leave yourself defenseless by turning your back toward the dog. Stop, stand your ground, look directly into the dogs eyes, and let him know that you are prepared to hurt him if he attacks

If a dog bothers you, stand your ground, look directly in the dog's eyes, and decide what course of action is safest.

you. Try not to be intimidated by the dog. Do not panic, decide what course of action is best for you. You may choose to slowly back away, but keep facing the dog. You may choose to slowly walk on by, but keep facing the dog. You may choose to pick up something to defend yourself, but keep facing the dog.

As a preventive measure you might want to carry something with you when you walk, such as a protective spray or a walking stick. One idea for a walking stick is the shaft of an old golf club with the head removed. It is light weight, sturdy, and fairly long. It is long enough to keep dogs away, has a handle, can be relatively sharp on the end, and can be used as a protective device as well as a walking stick.

Check the route you want to walk in a car before you walk it the first time. Walk in a group or carry some protection the first time you walk a new course. If there is an area where you want to walk and dogs are running loose, talk to the owners about tying them up or fencing them in. Most communities have a law against dogs running loose. If the owners are not cooperative call the dog catcher or the police. Do not give a dog the right to limit your use of public property.

The same dog should not bother you twice. If he does it is your fault for not doing something about it the first time.

If you walk at night, wear a reflective vest or tape.

Night Walking

It is safer to walk during the daylight hours. However, it is not possible for everyone to walk during the daytime, especially during the winter months when there are few daylight hours. If you must walk when it is dark consider the following suggestions to make it safer:

1. Wear light-colored clothing.
2. Wear a reflective vest or reflective tape on your clothing.
3. Walk in an area that has plenty of light.
4. Stay away from dark streets and alleys.
5. Walk with another person or a group.
6. Let someone know your exact route and what time you expect to be back.
7. Wear identification, including who should be called in case of an emergency and any medical conditions you have that might need to be known for proper emergency medical treatment.

Be especially cautious on potentially dangerous walking surfaces.

Walking Surfaces

Footing is an important consideration for fitness walkers. If you are unsure of a walking surface slow down and stay alert for dangerous spots.

When walking on pavement watch for holes and uneven cracks that might cause you to trip. On grass, gravel, and dirt roads watch for bumps, holes, and sudden differences in firmness. If you are walking indoors on a smooth surface, such as wood, be cautious of any wet spots, they can be extremely slippery. If you are walking on a wet or icy surface shorten your stride, keep your knees slightly bent, and use wider foot placement.

Overtraining

It is possible to get too much exercise. Exercise is a physical stressor that stimulates positive changes to take place in your body. However, if you exercise too much or too often, your body may not be able to recover. This can lead to muscle soreness, injury, illnesses, and burnout. Adequate rest and proper nutrition are essential to exercise progress and the development of physical fitness.

The following are some symptoms of overtraining:

sudden, unexpected weight loss
depression
insomnia
increased resting heart rate
decreased work capacity
poor performance
loss of enjoyment
loss of motivation

If you have several of these symptoms it is possible that you are overtraining. Try to get more rest between exercise sessions, watch your nutritional intake more closely, and reduce the intensity, duration, or frequency of your exercise. If the problem is overtraining you should start to feel better within a week or two.

Exercise may do more harm than good if you are overtraining. Each person has an individual rate at which they can best adapt to exercise. This is not a constant rate but one that changes continually and is influenced by the other stressors in your life. Although there are general guidelines for exercise, you need to listen carefully to your body to find the right amount for you.

Foot Care

The following tips will help you care for your feet:

1. Wear shoes that fit properly (see chapter 3).
2. Wear high quality shoes, which are better for your feet. Because they usually last longer they may not be any more expensive in the long run.
3. Wear comfortable socks of cotton or cotton blend material that will absorb moisture away from your skin.
4. Pay close attention to hot spots on your feet. Hot spots are the first stage of blisters.
5. Keep your feet clean and dry.
6. Keep your toenails trimmed properly.
7. If you have a foot problem go to a medical doctor who is a foot specialist.

Fitness Walking with Weights

Some fitness walkers use weights to increase the intensity of their workout. They generally add a weight vest, ankle weights, wrist weights, or hand weights. While this may not be a problem for the advanced fitness walker, it can be dangerous for the beginner. The additional weight can interfere with the natural walking rhythm, can cause unnecessary muscle soreness, and can produce an exercise load that is too great for the untrained heart.

Walking with weights.

Air Pollution

For many people in the United States air pollution is becoming a serious health problem and exercise hazard. If possible, try to do your fitness walking in an area that has clean air. Air pollution can irritate your lungs and aggravate respiratory conditions such as asthma and bronchitis.

Noise Pollution

Noise pollution may cause additional stress, negating the psychological benefits of fitness walking. Avoid heavy construction sites, congested streets, and large airports. Plan to walk in parks, on running tracks, in quiet neighborhoods, on country roads, or some other quiet place.

Fitness walking has many benefits that can improve the quality, and perhaps the length, of your life. However, it is necessary to take some precautions to make sure your fitness walking program remains safe, enjoyable, and beneficial.

Warm-Up, Cool Down, and Flexibility

5

Warm-Up

Always warm up before fitness walking. A good warm-up can improve your performance and reduce your risk of injury. A proper warm-up for fitness walking will require at least five to ten minutes. It should include gentle stretching and slow walking.

Stretching during the warm-up portion of your workout should be done gently and carefully. Vigorous stretching of cold muscles can result in injury and muscle soreness. Stretch each joint and major muscle group through a full range of motion.

The walking portion of your warm-up should start slowly and gradually increase in speed. Your walking motion will become smoother and easier as your muscles and joints respond to the warm-up.

Warm-up exercises increase muscle temperature and allow your heart rate to increase gradually up to your exercise heart rate. This is a safety measure to avoid unnecessary cardiac strain.

A traditional method of warming up is to perform gentle stretching first, then walking. Another method is to walk slowly for two to five minutes to warm the muscles and joints before stretching. Whether you prefer to do your warm-up walking first, or your stretching first, is a matter of personal preference. Both of these methods of warming up are effective. The key is to start slowly, and gradually warm up, before performing vigorous physical activity.

The warm-up period is also a time to get your mind ready for exercise. It is a time to focus your attention on your workout and on the development of your body. It is a time to think about your exercise goals and what you need to do during this exercise session to help you reach those goals. Exercise is more enjoyable and more effective if you have the proper mental attitude for your training session. While you are warming up, think positive thoughts about your workout and rededicate yourself to your exercise goals.

A good warm-up should prepare you physically and mentally for the aerobic portion of your workout.

Group warm-up.

Cool Down

The cool down is often the most neglected portion of a workout. Many exercisers skip this part of the exercise session. They think that the important part of the workout is finished and the cool down doesn't really matter. Nothing could be farther from the truth.

In aviation approximately 98 percent of all accidents occur during takeoff or landing. In general, the same is true of exercise. The extremely small percentage of heart attacks that have been associated with exercise seem to have occurred as a result of inadequate warm-up or cool down. In contrast an extremely large percentage of heart attacks that occur in the United States each year occur during the following activities: watching television, engaging in conversation, or lying in bed.

During the walking portion of your cool down there should be a gradual reduction in your walking speed. This will result in a gradual reduction in oxygen demand that will allow your heart to slowly return toward its resting rate.

The rhythmic contractions of your skeletal muscles help your heart to maintain adequate circulation during exercise. As your skeletal muscles contract rhythmically during walking, your veins are alternately squeezed and released. This milking action forces the blood in your veins to move toward your heart. Your blood doesn't flow back in the other direction because of blood pressure, and because of one-way valves in the veins that only allow blood flow toward your heart.

Rhythmic skeletal muscle contractions provide as much as 30 percent of the force necessary to circulate your blood during vigorous physical activity. If you are exercising vigorously, and stop suddenly, these important rhythmic muscle contractions also stop. Blood tends to accumulate in your veins, especially in your legs. Your heart must suddenly supply 100 percent of the force necessary for circulation. This is a very sudden increase in work load for your heart at a time when there is less blood returning to it. Therefore, it is recommended that you continue walking for a few minutes after the aerobic portion of your workout while gradually reducing your walking speed.

Your cool down should generally last at least five to ten minutes. It should include slow walking and stretching. The length of your cool down will depend on how vigorously you have been exercising and what physical condition you are in. The more vigorous the exercise and the less fit you are, the longer it takes to cool down.

Flexibility

Flexibility is the amount of movement, or range of motion, you have at each joint. Limited range of motion of a joint can limit your performance in some activities and will increase your risk of soft tissue injury. Increased flexibility is a healthy goal for most people.

Stretching to improve flexibility is best done after the aerobic portion of your workout when the soft tissues (muscles, tendons, and ligaments) are warm and the joints are well lubricated.

Static stretching is recommended for the following reasons:

It is an effective method of increasing flexibility.
There is less risk of injury to the soft tissues that are being stretched.
It helps prevent muscle soreness.
It may help relieve muscle soreness.
It is easy to learn.
It can be done without a partner.

General Tips for Stretching to Increase Flexibility

1. Use static stretch. To perform a static stretch, move a joint to the limit of its normal range of motion. Then, gently apply pressure to move the joint slightly beyond the point where it normally stops. Hold this position. Do not bounce.
2. Stretch to the point of moderate discomfort. You should be able to feel which muscle or group of muscles is being stretched but it should not be painful. Hold this position.
3. Hold each static stretch for ten to thirty seconds. Repeat each stretch one to three times.
4. Do not injure the soft tissues. You should not experience extreme discomfort or pain while stretching. If you experience extreme pain you are stretching too far.

5. Breathe slowly, rhythmically, and comfortably while stretching. Do not hold your breath. If you cannot breathe normally while stretching you are probably stretching too far.
6. Stretch any time you feel tightness. Stretching does not have to be restricted to your workout.
7. Warm-up stretches with cold muscles and joints should be light and easy.
8. Be sure your muscles are completely warmed up before performing stretching exercises to increase flexibility. Walk for a few minutes after you have completed the aerobic portion of your workout to allow your heart rate to return toward a resting level. Then stretch your muscles. They will stay warm for a long time after exercise.
9. Make stretching a relaxing daily habit. Some people like to stretch when they get up in the morning. It makes them feel better. Some people like to stretch before going to bed at night. It helps them relax and sleep better. Some people stretch before and after their daily exercise. It improves their performance and reduces their risk of injury.

Ten Stretches for Fitness Walking

1. Anterior Shoulder Stretch—Start in a standing position. With your hands behind your back, join the fingers of both hands together. Straighten both arms and raise your hands as high as possible behind your back. Hold this position.
2. Posterior Shoulder Stretch—Start in a standing position. Place your right arm overhead with your elbow bent. Grasp your right elbow with your left hand and gently pull your right elbow and upper arm behind your head. Hold this position. Repeat this exercise with the left arm.
3. Side Stretch—Stand with your feet shoulder width apart. Place both arms straight above your head and lean to the left. Stretch all of the muscles along the right side of your body. Hold this position. Repeat this exercise leaning to the right.
4. Adductor Stretch—Start in a standing position. Assume a straddle position with your feet apart, approximately three times your shoulder width. Bend your right knee slightly and stretch the muscles along the inside of your left thigh. Hold this position. Repeat this exercise with your left knee slightly bent and stretch the muscles along the inside of your right thigh.
5. Lunge Stretch—From a standing position take a large step forward. Bend the knee of your forward leg. Keep your feet pointed straight ahead. With your upper body erect and your arms out to the sides for balance, slowly press down and forward with your hips, stretching the muscles that cross the front of the hip joint. Bring your arms back, stretching the shoulder muscles at the same time. Hold this position. Repeat this exercise using the opposite leg.

Anterior shoulder stretch.

Posterior shoulder stretch.

Side stretch.

Adductor stretch.

Lunge stretch.

6. Hamstring Stretch—Start in a position lying on your back with your knees bent and both feet flat on the floor. Raise your right leg with your knee bent. Grasp the ball of the right foot with your right hand. Place your left hand behind your right knee. Pull your right thigh toward your chest while trying to straighten your leg at the knee. Hold this position. Repeat this exercise using the opposite leg.

7. Low Back Stretch—Start in a position lying on your back with both legs straight. Pull one thigh toward your chest with your knee bent and both hands behind your thigh. Hold this position. Repeat this exercise using the opposite leg.

8. Knees to Chest Stretch—Start in a position lying on your back with your knees bent and both feet flat on the floor. Bring both knees toward your chest. Grasp the back of both thighs and pull your knees toward your chest while curling your upper body forward. Hold this position.

9. Calf Stretch—Start in a standing position, place one foot about two or three feet in front of the other foot. Keep your back leg straight and the heel of your back foot flat on the floor. Your back foot should be pointing straight ahead. You should feel the stretch in the ankle and the back of the lower leg. Hold this position.

10. Ankle Circle Stretch—Stand on your left foot. Rotate your right foot at the ankle going clockwise, then counterclockwise, three times in each direction. Repeat this exercise with the left foot.

Hamstring stretch.

Low back stretch.

Knees-to-chest stretch.

Calf stretch.

Ankle circle stretch.

Warm-up, cool down, and flexibility are important components of your fitness walking program. All three contribute to greater safety and improved performance.

Activity 5a

The purpose of this activity is for you to learn flexibility exercises that may be used as part of your fitness walking program.

Perform each of the ten fitness walking stretches in chapter 5 following the general tips for stretching that are also in this chapter.

Fitness Walking Test

6

What is your present cardiovascular fitness level? Do you know? Have you measured it? Would you like to know? Would you like to measure it? There is now a walking test that can be used to measure your cardiovascular fitness level. The Rockport Fitness Walking Test is a scientifically validated field test of cardiovascular fitness using walking.

Knowing your current fitness level can help you find a realistic place to start your fitness walking program. By starting at the appropriate exercise level your walking program will be safer, more productive, and more enjoyable.

If you have not exercised in a long time be very cautious about taking any fitness test. Do not push yourself too hard during the test. It is much safer to complete the test comfortably and be classified in a lower fitness category than to push yourself too hard and risk injury. Some experts recommend beginning with a low-intensity starter program for at least two or three weeks before taking any fitness test.

Many people start exercise programs every year with unrealistic expectations. They start out highly motivated and full of enthusiasm but with little knowledge of their present fitness level or how much exercise they need. Consequently, they frequently start out doing too much. This often leads to muscle soreness, extreme fatigue, frustration, injury, or burnout. As a result most of these people lose their motivation and quit exercising.

It is unrealistic to think you can make up for years of bad habits in a few days. The benefits of regular exercise come from a lifelong habit of moderate exercise. It is better to start at a comfortable level of fitness walking, and enjoy it for the rest of your life, than to exercise at a high level for a few days and quit.

To prevent this from occuring, test yourself. This will enable you to start out on a fitness walking program that will best fit your needs and present physical condition. You will be able to enjoy your walking program while you progress gradually and safely.

Medical Clearance

Before taking the fitness walking test make sure it is medically safe for you to participate. Read the medical clearance section in chapter 4 and complete activity 4a before taking the Rockport Fitness Walking Test.

Use either the carotid artery or radial artery to count your pulse.

Why the Rockport Fitness Walking Test?

Researchers at the University of Massachusetts Medical School found that cardiovascular fitness could be estimated fairly accurately using four factors: age, sex, time to walk one mile, and heart rate at the completion of a one mile walk.

The researchers developed charts for estimating your cardiovascular fitness level using these four factors and fitness norms from the American Heart Association. This field test of cardiovascular fitness is called the Rockport Fitness Walking Test.

How to Take the Rockport Fitness Walking Test

To take the Rockport Fitness Walking Test you need to be able to count your heart rate. Gently place the finger tips of your index finger and middle finger on the radial artery. You will find this artery on the palm side of your forearm just above your wrist. You can also count your pulse by placing the same two fingertips on the carotid artery. You will find this artery by placing your finger tips along the side of your trachea near the top.

To take the walking test you need a watch that can measure your time in minutes and seconds. Find a flat measured mile to walk. The quarter-mile track at a local school is an excellent place. If there is not a track available, measure a one-mile course where you can walk continuously and uninterrupted. Avoid traffic and stoplights. It is a good idea to measure a half mile so you can walk out and back. That way you will know when you are halfway through the test and you will end up back where you started.

Walk the mile as fast as you can—running is not allowed. However, safety first, do not endanger your health. Slow down if the pace is too severe.

To determine your current fitness level two measurements are necessary. One is the time it takes you to walk one mile to the nearest second. The other is your heart rate immediately after finishing the mile.

When you cross the finish line record your time in minutes and seconds. Within five seconds after you finish locate your pulse and count the number of pulse beats in fifteen seconds. Multiply this number times four to get your exercise heart rate in beats per minute. The reason for locating your pulse immediately and taking a short fifteen second pulse count is to find your exercise heart rate. A great deal of recovery can occur within the first minute after you stop exercising. Therefore, if you wait too long to locate your pulse, or take a longer count, your test results will not be valid.

How to Find Your Fitness Category

Once your results are recorded you can determine your current fitness level by looking at the appropriate fitness level chart for your age and sex. The twenty- to twenty-nine-year-old relative fitness charts can be used for individuals under the age of twenty.

On the horizontal line at the bottom of the chart locate your time to complete the one-mile walk. Place a mark on the line at that point. On the vertical line at the left side of the chart locate your exercise heart rate in beats per minute. Draw a line straight up from your time and another line straight across from your heart rate. The point at which the two lines intersect will indicate your cardiovascular fitness level.

Retesting

How often should you retest yourself on the Rockport Fitness Walking Test? Ide- ally, it would be best to wait until you finish each twenty-week fitness walking program. The most important benefits come from a consistent and lifelong fitness walking program. By retesting yourself too frequently the tendency is to focus your attention on short-term changes. Although short-term changes are inter- esting, the long-term benefits are more important.

When you retest after completing a twenty-week fitness walking program, you may find that you have moved up to another fitness level. If that is the case, plan your next fitness walking program based on your new fitness level.

When you reach the point where you are satisfied with your cardiovascular fitness level, change to a maintenance walking program. Taking the walking test two or three times a year should be sufficient once you are on a maintenance program. However, there are some regular walkers who prefer to take the test once a month. This helps them monitor their fitness level on a regular basis and provides motivation for them to keep up with their exercise program.

Activity 6a

The purpose of this activity is to learn how to count your pulse at the radial artery and the carotid artery.

You need to know how to count your pulse before taking the Rockport Fitness Walking Test. Read or review the section in chapter 6 that explains how to count your pulse to determine your heart rate.

Find your pulse within five seconds and count it for fifteen seconds.

Practice three times using the radial artery and three times using the carotid artery.

To convert your pulse count to heart rate in beats per minute, multiply each fifteen-second count by four.

Activity 6b

The purpose of this activity is to determine your current fitness level using the Rockport Fitness Walking Test. Make sure you have read the medical and safety guidelines before taking the test.

Follow the directions for the Rockport Fitness Walking Test. When you finish record your results. Once your results are recorded, follow the directions in chapter 6 to find your fitness category.

Age _____   Sex _____

One Mile Walk Time in Minutes and Seconds _____

Exercise Heart Rate, 15 Seconds _____ × 4 = _____ BPM

Fitness Category _____

15 min

$$\begin{array}{r} 33 \\ \times\ 4 \\ \hline 132 \end{array}$$

20-29

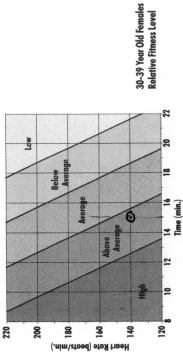

20-29 Year Old Males
Relative Fitness Level

20-29 Year Old Females
Relative Fitness Level

30-39

30-39 Year Old Males
Relative Fitness Level

30-39 Year Old Females
Relative Fitness Level

Relative Fitness Level Charts.

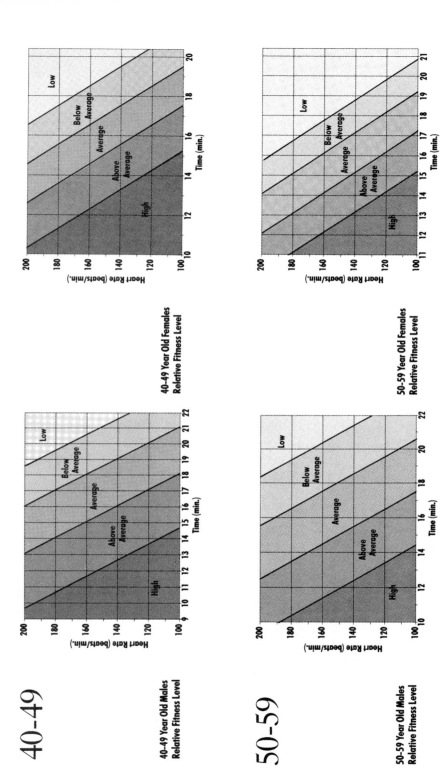

40-49

**40-49 Year Old Males
Relative Fitness Level**

**40-49 Year Old Females
Relative Fitness Level**

50-59

**50-59 Year Old Males
Relative Fitness Level**

**50-59 Year Old Females
Relative Fitness Level**

Relative Fitness Level Charts

60+

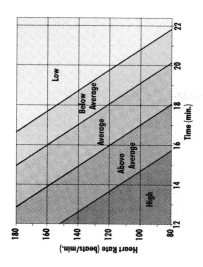

**60 + Year Old Males
Relative Fitness Level**

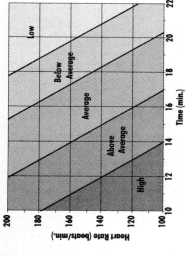

**60 + Year Old Females
Relative Fitness Level**

Relative Fitness Level Charts

Fitness Walking Programs

7

Exercise is like medicine. Both can be good for you if you get the right kind and the right amount. Fitness walking is the right kind of exercise for most people. This chapter will help you select the right amount.

Rockport Walking Programs

If you have completed the Rockport Fitness Walking Test you are ready to select your fitness walking program. The Rockport Walking Programs correspond to your current cardiovascular fitness level as measured by the Rockport Fitness Walking Test.

Find the appropriate exercise program chart for your age and sex. The twenty- to twenty-nine-year-old exercise program charts can be used for individuals under the age of twenty.

On the horizontal line at the bottom of the chart, locate your time to complete the one-mile walk. Place a mark on the line at that point. On the vertical line at the left side of the chart, locate your exercise heart rate at the end of the one-mile walk. Draw a line straight up from your time and another line straight across from your heart rate. The point at which the two lines intersect will indicate which exercise program is appropriate for you based on your current fitness level.

Rockport Exercise Programs

These programs were developed using extensive field data by the cardiologists and exercise scientists from the Exercise Physiology Lab and Department of Exercise Science at the University of Massachusetts Medical School. They are designed to help maintain or improve your level of fitness, depending on your current level. For best results, follow the programs closely.

At the end of each twenty-week period, retake the Rockport Fitness Walking Test to determine your new fitness level and exercise program.

On each program you'll see columns labeled "Pace" and "Heart Rate." The pace listed is only an approximation. Walking speed should be the pace that keeps your heart rate at the appropriate percentage listed. To estimate your maximum heart rate, subtract your age from 220.   = 183

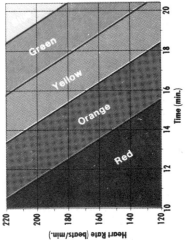

20-29 Year Old Males
Exercise Program

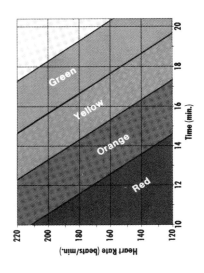

20-29 Year Old Females
Exercise Program

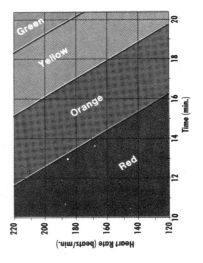

30-39 Year Old Males
Exercise Program

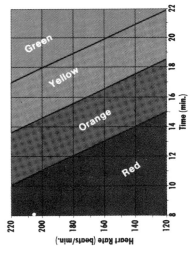

30-39 Year Old Females
Exercise Program

Exercise Program Charts.

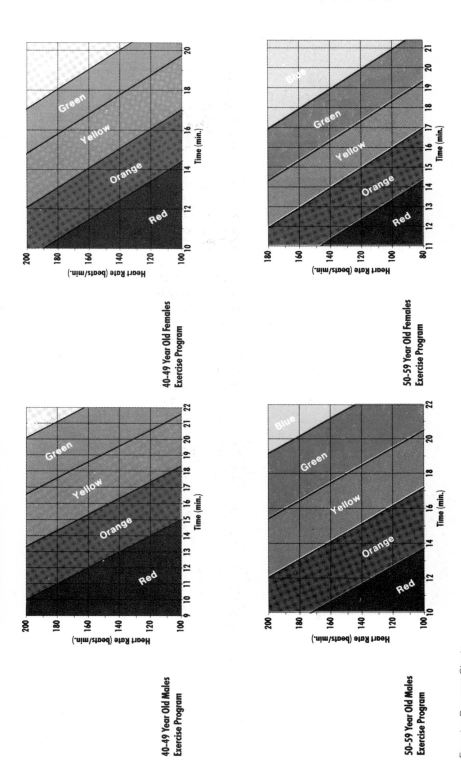

40-49 Year Old Females
Exercise Program

40-49 Year Old Males
Exercise Program

50-59 Year Old Females
Exercise Program

50-59 Year Old Males
Exercise Program

Exercise Program Charts.

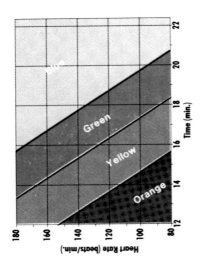

**60 + Year Old Females
Exercise Program**

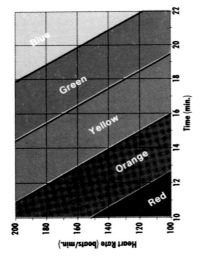

**60 + Year Old Males
Exercise Program**

Exercise Program Charts

Table 7.1   Low-Level Fitness Program. (Blue)

Week	Warm-up	Mileage	Pace (mph)	Heart Rate (% of max.)	Cool Down	Frequency (times per week)
1	5–7 mins. before-walk stretches	1.0	3.0	60	5–7 mins. after-walk stretches	5
2	5–7 mins.	1.0	3.0	60	5–7 mins.	5
3	5–7 mins.	1.25	3.0	60	5–7 mins.	5
4	5–7 mins.	1.25	3.0	60	5–7 mins.	5
5	5–7 mins.	1.5	3.0	60	5–7 mins.	5
6	5–7 mins.	1.5	3.5	60–70	5–7 mins.	5
7	5–7 mins.	1.75	3.5	60–70	5–7 mins.	5
8	5–7 mins.	1.75	3.5	60–70	5–7 mins.	5
9	5–7 mins.	2.0	3.5	60–70	5–7 mins.	5
10	5–7 mins.	2.0	3.75	60–70	5–7 mins.	5
11	5–7 mins.	2.0	3.75	70	5–7 mins.	5
12	5–7 mins.	2.25	3.75	70	5–7 mins.	5
13	5–7 mins.	2.25	3.75	70	5–7 mins.	5
14	5–7 mins.	2.5	3.75	70	5–7 mins.	5
15	5–7 mins.	2.5	4.0	70	5–7 mins.	5
16	5–7 mins.	2.5	4.0	70	5–7 mins.	5
17	5–7 mins.	2.75	4.0	70–80	5–7 mins.	5
18	5–7 mins.	2.75	4.0	70–80	5–7 mins.	5
19	5–7 mins.	3.0	4.0	70–80	5–7 mins.	5
20	5–7 mins.	3.0	4.0	70–80	5–7 mins.	5

At the end of the twenty-week fitness walking protocol, retest yourself to establish your new program.

Table 7.2   Below-Average Level Fitness Program. (Green)

Week	Warm-up	Mileage	Pace (mph)	Heart Rate (% of max.)	Cool Down	Frequency (times per week)
1	5–7 mins. before-walk stretches	1.5	3.0	60–70	5–7 mins. after-walk stretches	5
2	5–7 mins.	1.5	3.0	60–70	5–7 mins.	5
3	5–7 mins.	1.75	3.0	60–70	5–7 mins.	5
4	5–7 mins.	1.75	3.0	60–70	5–7 mins.	5
5	5–7 mins.	2.0	3.0	60–70	5–7 mins.	5
6	5–7 mins.	2.0	3.0	60–70	5–7 mins.	5
7	5–7 mins.	2.0	3.5	70	5–7 mins.	5
8	5–7 mins.	2.25	3.5	70	5–7 mins.	5
9	5–7 mins.	2.25	3.5	70	5–7 mins.	5
10	5–7 mins.	2.5	3.5	70	5–7 mins.	5
11	5–7 mins.	2.5	3.5	70	5–7 mins.	5
12	5–7 mins.	2.5	3.5	70	5–7 mins.	5
13	5–7 mins.	2.75	3.5	70	5–7 mins.	5
14	5–7 mins.	2.75	4.0	70–80	5–7 mins.	5
15	5–7 mins.	3.0	4.0	70–80	5–7 mins.	5
16	5–7 mins.	3.0	4.0	70–80	5–7 mins.	5
17	5–7 mins.	3.25	4.0	70–80	5–7 mins.	5
18	5–7 mins.	3.25	4.0	70–80	5–7 mins.	5
19	5–7 mins.	3.5	4.0	70–80	5–7 mins.	5
20	5–7 mins.	3.5	4.0	70–80	5–7 mins.	5

At the end of the twenty-week fitness walking protocol, retest yourself to establish your new program.

Table 7.3   Average-Level Fitness Program. (Yellow)

Week	Warm-up	Mileage	Pace (mph)	Heart Rate (% of max.)	Cool Down	Frequency (times per week)
1	5–7 mins. before-walk stretches	2.0	3.0	70	5–7 mins. after-walk stretches	5
2	5–7 mins.	2.25	3.0	70	5–7 mins.	5
3	5–7 mins.	2.5	3.0	70	5–7 mins.	5
4	5–7 mins.	2.5	3.0	70	5–7 mins.	5
5	5–7 mins.	2.75	3.0	70	5–7 mins.	5
6	5–7 mins.	2.75	3.5	70	5–7 mins.	5
7	5–7 mins.	2.75	3.5	70	5–7 mins.	5
8	5–7 mins.	2.75	3.5	70	5–7 mins.	5
9	5–7 mins.	3.0	3.5	70	5–7 mins.	5
10	5–7 mins.	3.0	3.5	70	5–7 mins.	5
11	5–7 mins.	3.0	4.0	70–80	5–7 mins.	5
12	5–7 mins.	3.0	4.0	70–80	5–7 mins.	5
13	5–7 mins.	3.25	4.0	70–80	5–7 mins.	5
14	5–7 mins.	3.25	4.0	70–80	5–7 mins.	5
15	5–7 mins.	3.5	4.0	70–80	5–7 mins.	5
16	5–7 mins.	3.5	4.5	70–80	5–7 mins.	5
17	5–7 mins.	3.5	4.5	70–80	5–7 mins.	5
18	5–7 mins.	4.0	4.5	70–80	5–7 mins.	5
19	5–7 mins.	4.0	4.5	70–80	5–7 mins.	5
20	5–7 mins.	4.0	4.5	70–80	5–7 mins.	5

At the end of the twenty-week fitness walking protocol you may either retest yourself and move to a new fitness walking category or begin the Average-Level Fitness Maintenance Program for a lifetime of fitness walking.

183 Heart Rate

Table 7.4 Above-Average Level Fitness Program (Orange)

Week	Warm-up	Mileage	Pace (mph)	Incline or Weight	Heart Rate (% of max.)	Cool Down	Frequency (times per week)
1	5–7 mins. before-walk stretches	2.5	3.5		70	5–7 mins. after-walk stretches	5 *128*
2	5–7 mins.	2.75	3.5		70	5–7 mins.	5
3	5–7 mins.	3.0	3.5		70	5–7 mins.	5
4	5–7 mins.	3.0	3.5		70	5–7 mins.	5
5	5–7 mins.	3.25	3.5		70	5–7 mins.	5
6	5–7 mins.	3.25	4.0		70–80	5–7 mins.	5
7	5–7 mins.	3.5	4.0		70–80	5–7 mins.	5
8	5–7 mins.	3.75	4.0		70–80	5–7 mins.	5
9	5–7 mins.	4.0	4.0		70–80	5–7 mins.	5
10	5–7 mins.	4.0	4.0		70–80	5–7 mins.	5
11	5–7 mins.	4.0	4.5		70–80	5–7 mins.	5
12	5–7 mins.	4.0	4.5		70–80	5–7 mins.	5
13	5–7 mins.	4.0	4.5		70–80	5–7 mins.	5
14	5–7 mins.	4.0	4.5		70–80	5–7 mins.	5
15	5–7 mins.	4.0	4.5	+	70–80	5–7 mins.	3
16	5–7 mins.	4.0	4.5	+	70–80	5–7 mins.	3
17	5–7 mins.	4.0	4.5	+	70–80	5–7 mins.	3
18	5–7 mins.	4.0	4.5	+	70–80	5–7 mins.	3
19	5–7 mins.	4.0	4.5	+	70–80	5–7 mins.	3
20	5–7 mins.	4.0	4.5	+	70–80	5–7 mins.	3

At the end of the twenty-week fitness walking protocol begin the Above-Average/High-Level Fitness Maintenance Program for a lifetime of fitness walking.

Table 7.5 High-Level Fitness Program. (Red)

Week	Warm-up	Mileage	Pace (mph)	Incline or Weight	Heart Rate (% of max.)	Cool Down	Frequency (times per week)
1	5–7 mins. before-walk stretches	3.0	4.0		70	5–7 mins. after-walk stretches	5
2	5–7 mins.	3.25	4.0	No	70	5–7 mins.	5
3	5–7 mins.	3.5	4.0	No	70	5–7 mins.	5
4	5–7 mins.	3.5	4.5	No	70–80	5–7 mins.	5
5	5–7 mins.	3.75	4.5	No	70–80	5–7 mins.	5
6	5–7 mins.	4.0	4.5	No	70–80	5–7 mins.	5
7	5–7 mins.	4.0	4.5	+	70–80	5–7 mins.	3
8	5–7 mins.	4.0	4.5	+	70–80	5–7 mins.	3
9	5–7 mins.	4.0	4.5	+	70–80	5–7 mins.	3
10	5–7 mins.	4.0	4.5	+	70–80	5–7 mins.	3
11	5–7 mins.	4.0	4.5	+	70–80	5–7 mins.	3
12	5–7 mins.	4.0	4.5	+	70–80	5–7 mins.	3
13	5–7 mins.	4.0	4.5	+	70–80	5–7 mins.	3
14	5–7 mins.	4.0	4.5	+	70–80	5–7 mins.	3
15	5–7 mins.	4.0	4.5	+	70–80	5–7 mins.	3
16	5–7 mins.	4.0	4.5	+	70–80	5–7 mins.	3
17	5–7 mins.	4.0	4.5	+	70–80	5–7 mins.	3
18	5–7 mins.	4.0	4.5	+	70–80	5–7 mins.	3
19	5–7 mins.	4.0	4.5	+	70–80	5–7 mins.	3
20	5–7 mins.	4.0	4.5	+	70–80	5–7 mins.	3

At the end of the twenty-week fitness walking protocol begin the Above-Average/High-Level Fitness Maintenance Program for a lifetime of fitness walking.

Yellow Maintenance Program

Warm-up: 5–7 minutes before-walk stretches

Aerobic workout: mileage: 4.0 pace: 4.5 mph

Heart rate: 70–80% of maximum

Cool down: 5–7 minutes after-walk stretches

Frequency: 3–5 times per week

Weekly mileage: 12–20 miles

Warm-up: 5–7 minutes before-walk stretches

Aerobic workout: mileage: 4.0 pace: 4.5 mph
weight/incline: add weights to upper body or add hill walking as needed to keep heart rate in target zone (70–80% of predicted maximum).

Heart rate: 70–80% of maximum

Cool down: 5–7 minutes after-walk stretches

Frequency: 3–5 times per week

Weekly mileage: 12–20 miles

Guidelines for Planning Your Own Personal Fitness Walking Programs

The preplanned Rockport Fitness Walking Programs are excellent. However, some fitness walkers may want to plan their own fitness walking program. The following guidelines will help you plan your own fitness walking program.

The Right Kind of Exercise

Why is fitness walking the right kind of exercise? The best type of exercise to develop your cardiovascular system, reduce your risk of cardiovascular disease, and reduce the amount of stored body fat you may have accumulated is some type of aerobic exercise. Aerobic exercises are those exercises that require you to use large amounts of oxygen for an extended period of time. Exercises that use large muscle groups in a rhythmic and continuous manner work best. Fitness walking is an excellent aerobic exercise.

The Right Amount of Exercise

The right amount of exercise is determined by its intensity, duration, and frequency.

Intensity

How fast do you need to walk? Intensity refers to how hard you need to exercise to benefit from each training session. Exercise heart rate provides a good indication of how hard you are exercising. A good guideline for fitness walking is to reach an exercise heart rate that is between 60 and 90 percent of your maximum heart rate. You can estimate your maximum heart rate by subtracting your age from 220.

Beginning fitness walkers should start out at a low intensity, 60 to 70 percent of their maximum heart rate. Only advanced fitness walkers should attempt to exercise at a high intensity, 80 to 90 percent of their maximum heart rate.

Activity 7a

The purpose of this activity is to determine your exercise heart rate range. This will help you monitor your exercise intensity.

Calculate your exercise heart rate range following the directions in chapter 7. _109.8 - 164.7_

Duration

How long do you need to walk? You should walk for fifteen to sixty minutes at your prescribed exercise heart rate. If you are just starting a fitness walking program keep the intensity low and the duration short. Gradually increase the duration first, then the intensity.

Frequency

How often should you walk? Fitness walking must be performed regularly to be effective. The recommended frequency for fitness walking is three to five days a week. Some people on a weight loss program may benefit from walking six or seven days a week but the risk of injury and burnout is higher.

Recovery

How much exercise is too much? As a general guideline, if you experience extreme muscle soreness the next day and could not repeat your fitness walking workout, you have done too much and need to reduce the amount of exercise the next time.

Exercise is only the stimulus for positive biological changes to occur in your body. These changes actually occur during the recovery time between exercise sessions. Make sure the exercise stimulus is not too severe and that you get adequate rest and nutrition between walking workouts.

Some people believe the old athletic myth of "no pain, no gain." They actually believe that you must exercise until you are in pain for exercise to be beneficial. Of course, this is one of the reasons they do not exercise regularly. Normally, people do not look forward to painful experiences and therefore avoid them.

A problem for some middle-aged people is that they want to get back into the physical condition they were in when they were young. This is not a realistic expectation.

Many people who have been inactive for a long time want to get in shape fast. Biological adaptation is a relatively slow process. You cannot expect to reverse the effects of years of sedentary living in a few days or weeks. These people often fall into the trap of thinking that if a little bit of exercise is good, then more must be better. This is only true to a point. Beyond that point additional exercise can be harmful. Follow the exercise guidelines. Progress slowly and safely. If you try to progress too quickly you are likely to become injured. If you are injured you are likely to lose your motivation to exercise. If you lose your motivation to exercise and quit, you will never achieve the benefits that come from regular exercise.

If you are exercising for your health you do not need to improve forever. When you reach the fitness level you want, change to a walking program that will keep you at that level.

These guidelines will help you select a safe and enjoyable walking program that you can stay with and benefit from for the rest of your life.

Because there is less to keep track of, some people prefer this program to the Rockport program. If you follow these guidelines, all you need to keep track of is your total minutes walked at your exercise heart rate. This method also gives you greater freedom to walk new courses, because you do not need to know the exact distance.

Guidelines for Fitness Walking to Develop Cardiovascular Fitness

The Right Kind of Exercise—Fitness Walking
The Right Amount of Exercise
    Intensity—60 to 90 percent of maximum heart rate
    Duration—15 to 60 minutes
    Frequency—3 to 7 days per week

The American Heart Association Walking Program

The American Heart Association offers a program that is excellent for beginners who are not regular exercisers. Each workout should consist of a warm-up, a walk within the target heart rate zone, and a cool down. You are to keep your exercise heart rate between 60 and 75 percent of your maximum heart rate and walk at least three times each week.

Table 7.6   American Heart Association Walking Program.

Week	Target Zone Exercising	Total Time in Minutes (warm-up + target zone exercising + cool down)
1	Walk briskly 5 min.	15 min.
2	Walk briskly 7 mins.	17 min.
3	Walk briskly 9 min.	19 min.
4	Walk briskly 11 min.	21 min.
5	Walk briskly 13 min.	23 min.
6	Walk briskly 15 min.	25 min.
7	Walk briskly 18 min.	28 min.
8	Walk briskly 20 min.	30 min.
9	Walk briskly 23 min.	33 min.
10	Walk briskly 26 min.	36 min.
11	Walk briskly 28 min.	38 min.
12	Walk briskly 30 min.	40 min.
13 on:	Check your pulse periodically to see if you are exercising within your target zone. As you get more in shape, try exercising within the upper range of your target heart zone. Remember that your goal is to continue getting the benefits you seek while enjoying your activity.	

Total Health-related Physical Fitness

Total health-related physical fitness includes cardiovascular endurance, muscle endurance, strength, flexibility, and body composition.

Cardiovascular Endurance

Cardiovascular endurance refers to your ability to continue vigorous total body activity for a relatively long period of time. To develop cardiovascular endurance, perform exercises that use large muscle groups in a rhythmic and continuous manner. Maintain an exercise heart rate that is 60 to 90 percent of your maximum heart rate for fifteen to sixty minutes, and repeat this workout three to seven times each week.

Muscle Endurance

Muscle endurance refers to the ability of individual muscles or muscle groups to exert force for many repetitions, or to hold a position for an extended period of time. To develop muscle endurance, perform exercises that require movement through a full range of motion against resistance. Use a resistance that is 50 to 70 percent of your maximum voluntary contraction (one repetition maximum) and execute twenty to thirty repetitions. Perform one to three sets of each exercise and repeat your muscle endurance exercises three to five days per week.

Strength

Strength refers to the amount of force a muscle can exert. To develop strength perform exercises that involve movement through a full range of motion against resistance. Use a resistance that is 70 to 100 percent of your maximum voluntary contraction (one repetition maximum) and execute one to ten repetitions. Perform each exercise for one to three sets and repeat your strength training program three days per week.

Flexibility

Flexibility refers to the range of motion available at a joint. To develop flexibility use slow static stretch exercises, stretch to the point of moderate discomfort, hold each stretch for ten to thirty seconds, perform each stretch one to three times, and repeat your stretching program three to seven days per week.

Body Composition

Body composition refers to what your body is composed of. The particular concern is how much of your body is stored body fat. The best exercises to reduce stored body fat are those that use large muscle groups in a rhythmic and continuous manner. Exercise at a heart rate that is 60 to 90 percent of your heart rate range for thirty to sixty minutes, and repeat this workout five to seven days per week.

Total Health-related Physical Fitness Program

Fitness walking programs, including the stretching exercises during the warm-up and cool down, develop cardiovascular endurance, muscle endurance, flexibility, and body composition. Adding a few strength exercises after the walking portion of your cool down and before the stretching portion of your cool down would result in a good total health-related physical fitness program.

Your total health-related physical fitness walking program would be as follows:

Warm-up stretching (very gentle stretch).
Warm-up walking.
Fitness walking at exercise heart rate.
Cool-down walking.
Strength and muscle endurance exercises.
Cool-down stretching (stretching to increase flexibility).

Fitness Walking Techniques

8

This chapter explains some specific walking techniques that will increase your speed, stride length, and efficiency. There should also be improvements in your balance, coordination, body control, posture, and agility as you learn these techniques.

Once you have learned the proper form, your pace will become faster. Your heart and lungs will have to work harder to supply the oxygen needed to the working muscles. This will improve your cardiovascular conditioning.

Even after you have learned these walking techniques and have become a regular fitness walker, you will need to return to this chapter to review the techniques and refine your walking skill. The most experienced fitness walkers continue to review and improve their walking techniques.

Learn one walking technique at a time. Focus on one technique during each workout. Practice each technique until it becomes automatic.

Technique 1: Posture and Alignment

For the smoothest walking motion, maintain correct posture and body alignment. Apply the guidelines in activity 8a while you walk.

Technique 1: Posture and alignment.

Activity 8a

The purpose of this activity is to learn correct body alignment for fitness walking.

Read technique one, posture and alignment. Assume a standing position with correct body alignment for fitness walking. Have a partner evaluate each guideline and place a check in either the yes or no column.

Guidelines	Yes	No
Head and neck erect	___	___
Eyes straight ahead	___	___
Shoulders pulled back and relaxed	___	___
Back straight	___	___
Chest lifted up	___	___
Abdomen pulled in	___	___
Buttocks tucked in	___	___
Elbows down at side	___	___
Elbows bent at 90-degree angle	___	___
Palms facing inward	___	___
Hands in relaxed fist position	___	___

Technique 2: Heel Contact

From a position of correct posture, swing one leg forward. Land on the outer edge of your heel with the bottom of your foot at about a forty-degree angle to the ground. Make sure your heel contacts the ground first. Do not land flat-footed or on the ball of your foot.

Activity 8b

The purpose of this activity is to emphasize the idea of landing on your heel first, as opposed to landing flat-footed or on the ball of your foot.

Read technique two, heel contact. Walk ten steps. Have a partner check to see if you are contacting the ground with your heel first. Your foot should also be at approximately a forty-degree angle to the ground when your heel makes contact.

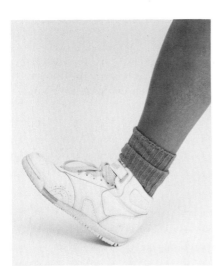

Technique 2: Heel contact.

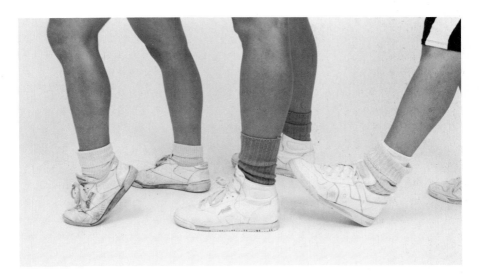

Technique 3: Heel-to-toe roll.

Technique 3: Heel-to-Toe Roll

Once your heel makes contact with the ground, begin to roll your foot forward, keeping your weight toward the outer edge of your foot until reaching your toes. The outer edge of your foot acts as a natural rocker bottom for continuous forward motion. As you roll your foot forward with your weight toward the outer edge, keep you knees pointing straight ahead.

Activity 8c

The purpose of this activity is to experience the heel-to-toe roll.

Read technique three, heel-to-toe roll. Walk ten steps. Have a partner watch your heel-to-toe roll. After your heel makes contact with the ground, roll your foot forward. Keep the weight toward the outer edge of your foot. Continue to roll forward until you push off with your toes.

Technique 4: Push Off

Following the heel-to-toe roll, continue your forward motion with a push off from your toes. Resist the temptation to pick your foot up early, as you might do in casual walking. Keep your foot in contact with the ground for as long as possible. You can lengthen your stride on each step by pushing off with your toes.

To reduce excessive side-to-side swaying and undue stress on your joints, keep your support foot pointing straight ahead. If your body rises and falls with each step, you may be pushing off from the front part of your foot instead of your toes. If this happens, reduce your speed and focus on the push off.

To receive the greatest benefits from fitness walking it is necessary to walk at a brisk pace. A longer stride will help you walk faster because you will be able to cover more ground in fewer steps.

You may need to perform stretching exercises to improve your ankle, foot, and toe flexibility for a greater range of motion on the push off.

Technique 4: Push off.

Technique 5: Foot placement.

Activity 8d

The purpose of this activity is to emphasize the push off.

Read technique four, push off. Raise yourself on the toes of both feet at the same time. Repeat this five times. Next, practice the push off by walking a short distance with an exaggerated push off. Push all the way up on your toes before breaking contact with the ground. Have a partner watch to see if you are pushing off with your toes or picking your foot up early.

Technique 5: Foot Placement

During brisk walking, each foot should be placed one or two inches to the side of an imaginary center line on the ground. Your feet and knees should be pointing as straight ahead as possible. This will help you walk in a straight line. When walking with weights or on rough terrain, you may need to use a wider foot placement.

As you bring your leg forward during the recovery phase, try to pull your leg straight forward. Your knee should pass beneath your hip joint. Your recovery leg should not brush against your support leg or swing way out to the side.

Activity 8e

The purpose of this activity is to practice proper foot placement for fitness walking.

Read technique five, foot placement. Have a partner observe from the front and the back while you walk along a straight line. As you walk, place each foot parallel to the line and about one or two inches to the side of the line.

Technique 6: Arm Swing

During fitness walking your arms should be bent at about a ninety-degree angle at the elbow joint. Your hands should be in a relaxed fist position with your palms facing inward. In this position your arms should swing forward and backward from the shoulder joint. Each arm should swing in a straight path and remain fairly close to your body to avoid side-to-side swaying of the upper body and hips. On the forward swing, your hand should rise at least to shoulder level. On the backswing, your elbow should rise as high as comfort will allow.

The arms play an important role in fitness walking. Your arms and legs are like teammates—the faster you swing your arms, the faster your legs will move.

Technique 6: Arm swing.

Activity 8f

The purpose of this activity is to focus your attention on your arm swing while fitness walking.

Read technique six, arm swing. Using proper posture and alignment, practice the arm swing in a standing position. Start slowly and gradually increase the speed of your arms.

Have a partner check to make sure your arm swing is correct.

Technique 7: Breathing

Your breathing usually takes place without conscious voluntary control. It automatically adjusts to your need for oxygen. You can regulate your breathing to a certain degree by assuming conscious control of the depth and rate. However, if your breathing gets too far out of line, your body will take over automatic control again.

If you start slowly and progress gradually, your breathing pattern will develop naturally, along with your other walking techniques. It should not require thought on your part.

Even though your breathing will automatically adjust to your need for oxygen, it is generally more comfortable if your breathing is coordinated with your arm and leg movements. There is no set pattern that is right for everyone, and there is no one pattern that will be right for every walking speed. Experiment with different speeds and breathing patterns until you find the ones most comfortable for you.

Activity 8g

The purpose of this activity is to help you think about rhythmic breathing.

Read technique seven, breathing. Begin walking at a slow pace. Try breathing in for three steps and out for three steps. Gradually increase your pace. At a faster walking pace try breathing in for two steps and out for two steps.

Be aware of your breathing. It should be rhythmic and comfortable. Don't try to control it too much. Your body will automatically regulate the depth and rate of your breathing to meet your oxygen demand.

Technique 8: Hip Movement

To increase your walking speed, you must increase the length of your stride. One way to increase stride length is to turn your hips and allow them to add to your leg movements. By allowing your hips to turn, your back leg can go farther back and your forward leg can go farther forward.

Keep your back foot in contact with the ground until you have full extension of your leg and you push off from your toes. When swinging your leg to the front, reach forward with your front foot as far as comfort will allow. This technique alone can add as much as eight inches to your stride length.

Using the hips more reduces the amount of up and down movement with each step, converting wasted vertical energy into useful horizontal energy. Also, the abdominal and hip muscles are exercised more vigorously with increased hip movement.

Activity 8h

The purpose of this activity is to increase your stride length.

Read technique eight, hip movement. From the ready position, take one giant step forward, extending your right leg as far forward as it will comfortably go. Hold this position for three seconds, then lift your right foot and move it another

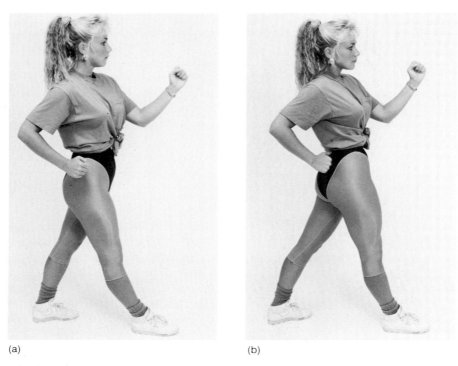

(a)   (b)

Technique 8: (a) Incorrect and (b) correct hip movement.

three to five inches forward. Hold this new position for ten seconds. Return to the ready position and repeat the procedure with your left leg. Perform this activity five times with each leg.

Have a partner measure your normal walking stride from the heel of your forward foot to the toes of your back foot. Then measure your stride after allowing your hips to follow through. Remember to keep your foot in contact with the ground as long as possible. Now compare the measurements to discover the extra distance in your stride length when you include the hip movement.

Technique 9: Leg Vault

Incorporating this technique into your walking movement will add even more forward drive to your push off. To perform this technique it is helpful to think of your support leg as a vaulting pole. Heel contact is the pole plant of fitness walking. Swing one leg forward. At the point of contact, your leg should be straight, but not rigidly locked into extension at the knee joint. The idea is to

Technique 9: Leg vault.

reach out with the front leg and make contact with the ground using the longest practical stride. Do not interpret this to mean you should drive your heel into the ground with a stiff leg.

Vault your body forward using your support leg as a vaulting pole. Your leg should be straight throughout the heel-to-toe roll and the push off. Finish the vaulting action with your leg extended and a final push off from your toes.

Activity 8i

The purpose of this activity is to emphasize the feeling of straightening your support leg.

Read technique nine, leg vault. Practice the robot walk by keeping your legs straight and using the heel-to-toe roll. Do not bend at the knee joint. In this exaggerated activity you will be able to notice how each leg acts like a vaulting pole.

Next, start walking in slow motion and stop just before you finish the push-off technique. Have a partner check to make sure your push-off leg is straight. Walk at progressively faster speeds and have your partner watch your push-off leg. Make sure there is no bend at the knee joint until the leg starts to swing forward during the recovery phase.

Technique 10: The race walk.

Technique 10: The Race Walk

This advanced technique requires accelerated arm and leg speed. In this technique you walk as fast as you possibly can. To walk faster, you must swing your arms and legs faster. This is an extremely tiring technique. You will need to gradually build up your time and distance using this all-out speed.

Race walking is not for beginners, it is for intermediate and advanced fitness walkers who want a higher intensity workout. High-intensity race walking could result in very sore muscles or injury for unconditioned beginners.

Activity 8j

The purpose of this activity is to learn how to add speed to your fitness walking. This technique is especially important if you plan to increase the intensity of your workouts.

Read technique ten, the race walk. After you have warmed up properly, and have walked for several minutes, move your arms and legs faster while you walk. Begin by race walking for short distances. Use a slower pace between these sprints for recovery. Gradually increase the distance you can race walk as you increase your cardiovascular endurance and leg strength.

Next, count the number of race-walk steps you can take in one minute. An easy way to find your steps per minute is to count how many steps you take with your right foot in one minute and multiply by two. This is much easier than trying to count every step when you are walking at very fast speeds. The maximum effective leg speed you will probably be able to achieve with a four-foot stride is about two hundred steps a minute. For most fitness walking workouts, a range of 130 to 180 steps a minute is good.

Fitness walking, like other sports and fitness activities, requires good technique for optimal performance. By focusing on one technique at a time and regular practice you will soon become a highly skilled fitness walker.

Tips for Higher Intensity Workouts

Once you have mastered the basic fitness walking techniques, and have developed your cardiovascular fitness to a high level, you may find it difficult to reach your training heart rate. Here are some ideas to help you increase the intensity of your fitness walking workouts once you have reached this advanced level of training. High-intensity workouts should not be used by unconditioned beginners.

Vigorous Arm Swings

Begin with your elbows bent at a ninety-degree angle, your fists relaxed, and your palms facing inward. Swing your arms in a straight path, forward and backward, keeping your arms in close to your body. Now, pump your arms more vigorously and add movement at the elbow joint. On the upswing pull your forearm toward your upper arm as far as it will go. On the downswing push your forearm back down to a ninety-degree angle at the elbow joint. You may even want to tighten and relax your fist with each arm swing.

The additional muscle contractions of the arms will increase your oxygen demand. The increased oxygen demand will cause your oxygen delivery system to work harder and result in a higher intensity workout.

Hill Walking

Hill walking will increase your exercise intensity and add variety to your walking routine. It will also improve your cardiovascular fitness level. Depending on the steepness of the hill, your heart rate will be ten to fifty beats per minute higher when walking uphill. This increase in exercise heart rate makes hill walking an excellent cardiovascular conditioner and a great calorie burner.

High arm swings.

Stair Walking

Stair walking is basically hill walking for those who do not have hills. It is a superb exercise for your cardiovascular system. In addition to the aerobic benefits, stair walking develops muscular strength in your legs and hips because your body weight must be lifted with each step. To increase your exercise intensity and to add variety to your fitness walking program, try stair walking.

Walking with Weights

An advanced fitness walker may wish to add hand weights or wrist weights to increase exercise intensity. When using hand weights and wrist weights, your arm swing should be a controlled movement. Hand weights should not make you feel unbalanced. Start off with one-pound weights and gradually increase as your conditioning improves.

Beginners are advised not to use weights at the start of their walking program.

Fitness Walking Techniques

1. Posture and Alignment
2. Heel Contact
3. Heel-to-Toe Roll
4. Push Off
5. Foot Placement
6. Arm Swing
7. Breathing
8. Hip Movement
9. Leg Vault
10. Race Walk

Nutrition

9

If you are like most Americans you are striving to eat better. It is a goal worth pursuing. This chapter will assist you in your quest for a healthier life-style through proper nutrition.

What Is Nutrition?

Nutrition includes the food you eat, its use within your body, and its relationship to your health. It involves the study of the major food components: carbohydrates, proteins, fats, vitamins, minerals, and water. Eating a well-balanced diet for good health is the goal of proper nutrition.

Nutrition and Good Health

To enjoy good health, proper nutrition is vital. It has a positive influence on the quality of your life and helps you stay energetic. Eating is more than just satisfying hunger. The food you ingest is important for feeding all the body's cells. Foods provide the body with nutrients that are essential for growth, repair, and regulation of body processes.

Poor health can result from overeating, undereating, or eating low-nutrient foods. Some of the serious health problems that are related to poor nutrition include heart disease, stroke, breast cancer for women, and prostate and colon cancer for men.

You may already know the association between nutrition and good health. Yet, sound nutrition is more than avoiding one harmful food or filling up on nutritious food. In order for good health to result, several types of food must work closely together.

The Basic Components of Food

Foods are composed of chemical compounds that supply energy. The energy value of food is measured in calories. If an apple contains 100 calories, it provides 100 units of energy. Carbohydrates and proteins each contain 4 calories per gram; fat contains 9 calories per gram. There are no calories in vitamins, minerals, or water.

Carbohydrates

Carbohydrates are an ideal fuel and contribute about half of the body's energy needs. They are also needed to utilize fat efficiently. The two major types of carbohydrates are starches and sugars.

Daily Carbohydrate Needs

Most nutrition experts believe you need at least 125 grams or 4½ ounces of carbohydrates daily. About 300 grams or 10½ ounces is probably ideal for most people. This translates into a minimum of four servings a day. A serving is equal to 1/2 cup or 1 slice. Nutritionists recommend that about 60 percent of your calories should come from carbohydrates.

Good Choices

Good choices for carbohydrates include legumes (dried beans and peas), oatmeal, brown rice, pasta, most fruits, whole grain bread, and starchy vegetables like potatoes and winter squash.

Choices to Limit

Choices to limit include sweetened cereals, french fries, white breads, rolls, donuts, pastries, and other white-flour baked goods.

Fats

A certain amount of fat is required for health. Fats (also known as *lipids*) provide energy, escort fat-soluble vitamins A, D, E, and K in the blood, cushion vital organs, insulate the body, are essential parts of every cell, and contribute to hormone synthesis and the blood clotting mechanism.

The two types of fats in foods are saturated and unsaturated. Saturated fats, except for the oils, come from animal sources and are solid at room temperature. They include meats, butter, whole milk, coconut oil, and palm oil. Unsaturated fats come from plant sources and are liquid at room temperature. Two classes of unsaturated fats are polyunsaturated (corn, soy, sunflower, and cottonseed oil) and monounsaturated (olive oil).

The average daily intake of fat in the American diet is about 40 percent of total calories. The American Heart Association recommends reducing fat intake to 30 percent, with saturated fat providing no more than 10 percent.

Fat and Cholesterol

Cholesterol is a waxy, fatlike substance that is essential for life. It is used to form cell membranes, the sex hormones estrogen and progesterone, and other vital substances. Cholesterol also ensures proper functioning of the nervous system. It is not a required nutrient because the body manufactures all the cholesterol it needs. Cholesterol is found in all animal foods, such as meat, eggs, fish, poultry, and dairy products.

Dietary cholesterol is usually stored in the liver, where it is either excreted or directed to the cells. Too much circulating blood cholesterol has been linked to coronary artery disease. Atherosclerosis occurs when excess cholesterol builds up in the bloodstream and attaches itself to the walls of the blood vessels. Blood cholesterol is the major ingredient in fatty plaque. When fatty plaque develops in the coronary arteries, it decreases the flow of blood and promotes the growth of blood clots. Over time, this might cut off the flow of blood. In the coronary arteries this can lead to a heart attack. In the cerebral arteries in the brain, this process can lead to a stroke.

A healthy recommendation is to decrease your intake to no more than 100 milligrams of cholesterol per 1,000 calories, with a maximum of 300 milligrams daily (equivalent to about one egg yolk).

Positive dietary and life-style changes can prevent plaque from building up in the coronary arteries. Recently, scientists have also found that positive life-style changes (low-fat diet, no smoking, regular exercise) can reduce the plaque already present and thus widen the narrowed coronary arteries. This is an exciting new finding in the treatment of coronary artery disease.

Types of Cholesterol

Cholesterol is carried in the bloodstream by lipoproteins, including the following two types:

1. Low-density lipoproteins (LDL), or "bad cholesterol," are believed to deposit cholesterol on artery walls, potentially causing coronary artery disease.
2. High-density lipoproteins (HDL), or "good cholesterol," are thought to remove cholesterol from artery walls and transport it back to the liver for processing or removal.

Who's at risk?

These are the latest recommendations for adults from the National Cholesterol Education Program.

	Total Cholesterol (mg/dl)	LDL (mg/dl)
Desirable	under 200	under 130
Borderline-high	200–239	130–159
High	240 or more	160 or more

An estimated 25 percent of all Americans have high cholesterol and another 25 percent are borderline-high. Have you had your blood cholesterol levels checked recently? If not, make an appointment with your physician. Ask to receive a complete lipid profile, usually LDL, HDL, and triglycerides (another form of fats in the bloodstream.) See table 9.1 for cholesterol-, LDL-, and HDL-lowering strategies.

Table 9.1   Strategies for Lowering Total Cholesterol, Lowering LDL, and Increasing HDL.

1. Lose body fat, if you're overfat.
2. Reduce dietary cholesterol.
3. Reduce saturated fat intake.
4. Exercise regularly.
5. Stop smoking.
6. Eat more soluble fiber.
7. Follow the advice of your physician.

Omega-3 Fatty Acids

Omega-3 fatty acids are unique polyunsaturated fats found in deep sea fish. They are showing promise in preventing and treating cardiovascular disease. Evidence suggests these fish contain polyunsaturated fats that may lower total cholesterol and LDL cholesterol, and raise the good (HDL) cholesterol level. Omega-3 fatty acids may reduce blood clotting by thinning the blood. This, in turn, decreases platelets sticking to each other and to the blood vessels, which lessens the likelihood of a heart attack due to a blood clot in the coronary arteries.

Fish containing omega-3 fatty acids have also been found to lower triglycerides, and perhaps prevent hardening of the arteries (arteriosclerosis). Fish high in omega-3s include mackerel, lake trout, herring, fresh albacore tuna, sablefish, sturgeon, whitefish, salmon, anchovies, and halibut (see table 9.2).

At this time, most experts recommend fish over fish oil supplements. Fish is one of the best foods available in the American diet. Besides its protective oil, fish is rich in protein, iron, B vitamins, and other nutrients, and it can replace meats high in saturated fat.

In case you are not a fish lover, the good news is you don't have to eat big amounts of fish to improve your cardiovascular health. Recent evidence suggests two to three servings a week are adequate.

Good Choices for Fat

Olive, corn, safflower, sunflower, and other liquid vegetable oils are good choices. Fish with omega-3 fatty acids are also a good choice.

Choices to Limit

Limit your intake of butter, lard, palm oil, and coconut oil. Palm oil and coconut oil are found in commercial pastry and nondairy creamers. Also limit the fat in meat and dairy products.

Proteins

Proteins are known as the building blocks of the body. They are commonly found in meat, eggs, fish, and dairy products. Proteins are needed for growth, repair, and maintenance of all body cells. They also transmit hereditary characteristics and help form the hormones and enzymes used to regulate body processes.

Table 9.2   Omega-3 Fatty Acids.

Species (italic indicates fish with at least one gram of Omega-3 fatty acids.)	Percent of Calories from Fat	Omega-3 Fatty Acids (grams per 4 oz.)	Species (italic indicates fish with at least one gram of Omega-3 fatty acids.)	Percent of Calories from Fat	Omega-3 Fatty Acids (grams per 4 oz.)
Haddock	7	0.2	Channel Catfish	30	0.7
Cod	8	0.3	*Rainbow Trout*	31	1.2
Pollack	9	0.6	*Oyster, Pacific*	31	1.0
Northern Pike	9	0.2	Carp	33	0.3
Sole	9	0.3	Oyster, Eastern	34	0.5
Tuna, light in water	10	0.2	Salmon, Atlantic	35	0.4
Scallop	11	0.4	*Salmon, Pink*	36	2.2
Crab	11	0.5	*Salmon, Sockeye, canned*	36	1.8
Red Snapper	11	0.4	*Whitefish, Lake*	37	1.0
Lobster	11	0.3	*Herring, Atlantic*	43	1.3
Shrimp	12	0.5	*Salmon, Coho, canned*	45	1.8
Flounder	13	0.3	*Mackerel, Atlantic*	52	2.5
Turbot	13	0.3	Lake Trout	54	N.A.
Tuna, white in water	14	0.5	*Salmon, Chinook, canned*	57	3.3
Rockfish	14	0.6	*Salmon, Chinook*	59	2.4
Halibut, Pacific	17	0.4	*Sablefish*	68	1.7
Clam	17	0.2	*American Eel*	71	1.9
Striped Bass	19	0.9	For Comparisons:		
Squid	20	1.0	Chicken breast, no skin	19	0.03
Mussel	21	0.8	Round steak, lean	29	trace
Ocean Perch	23	0.5	Ground beef	64	trace
Whiting	26	N.A.			
Porgy	27	N.A.			

N.A. = Not available
All values are for cooked fish, meat, and poultry.
Copyright 1987, Center for Science in the Public Interest.
Source: Decisions for Health, Clinte, Breuss and Glenn E. Richardson, (Dubuque, Iowa: Wm. C. Brown Publishers, 1989).

   Protein is made up of twenty-two different amino acids. It is essential that eight of these amino acids be included in your diet because your body cannot produce them. All twenty-two amino acids must be present in your body at the same time to form protein.

   One way to get all of the amino acids you need is to include foods from animal sources in your daily diet. The protein in these foods is known as complete protein because it includes all eight of the essential amino acids.

   Incomplete protein comes from plant foods (vegetables and grains) and lacks one or more of the essential amino acids. However, you can form complete proteins by combining plant proteins with each other or with animal protein. Common examples include: cereal and milk, rice and beans, macaroni and cheese, and peanut butter on whole wheat bread.

Protein Needs

Many Americans take in more proteins than they need. Only about 12 percent of your total daily calories should come from protein. A simple way to get a rough estimate of your protein needs is take your weight and divide by three. If you weigh 150 pounds, your approximate daily protein needs would be 50 grams.

Good Choices

Poultry without skin, fish, shellfish, and lean red meat are good choices of complete protein.

Choices to Limit

Fatty red meat (prime rib, filet mignon, spareribs, lamb), organ meats, and processed meats such as salami, bologna, hot dogs, and sausage should be limited.

Vitamins

Vitamins are organic substances needed in very small amounts by the body. Although vitamins do not supply energy, they help release the energy from carbohydrates, fats, and proteins. For example, vitamin D is necessary for calcium to become part of the bone structure. Vitamins also help with other chemical reactions in the body.

Most people will receive all the vitamins they need by eating a variety of foods. A majority of the American population believe they need daily vitamin supplements to maintain health, prevent ailments, and increase energy levels. Billions of dollars are spent each year on vitamin pills and tonics that are questionable and could actually be dangerous.

A single balanced vitamin-mineral pill is recommended if you are following a restricted diet, below 1500 calories a day. A multivitamin supplement could be beneficial if you are not eating a well-balanced diet.

Minerals

Minerals, like vitamins, are also needed in small amounts and do not supply energy. They have many functions, from building strong bones and teeth to forming hemoglobin in red blood cells. Besides assisting in nerve transmission and muscle contraction, minerals also help regulate fluid levels and the acid-base balance of the body.

Iron, zinc, selenium, copper, cobalt, and manganese are known as trace minerals because they are needed only in small amounts. Major minerals are required in much larger quantities, such as calcium, phosphorous, potassium, and magnesium. Because minerals are absorbed, utilized, and eliminated by the body, they must be replaced on a daily basis.

Eating a wide variety of foods is the best way to obtain sufficient quantities of the essential minerals. Fruits and vegetables are ideal sources for minerals.

Water

Water is often called the "forgotten nutrient." It may be our most important nutrient, because without water we would not live more than a week. Over half of our body weight is water. Water provides the medium for nutrient and waste transport and plays a vital role in nearly all of our bodies biochemical reactions.

People seldom think about the importance of an adequate daily intake of water. Adults require eight glasses of water a day, depending on their exercise levels and environment. If you drink beverages that tend to dehydrate the body (tea, coffee, and alcohol), you should increase your water consumption. Strained, uncomfortable bowel movements may be caused by an inadequate daily intake of water. The average American drinks more soft drinks in a year than water.

Good choices for water intake are plain water from the tap and any kind of mineral water or bottled water. Choices to limit include sweetened soda, coffee, and alcohol.

Fiber: A Key Nonnutritive Food Component

Although fiber does not produce calories or energy for the body, it is an important substance in the diet. Known as *roughage* and *bulk,* fiber is made up of indigestible carbohydrates. It consists mainly of the cellulose that is part of fruits, vegetables, and grains.

There are two types of fiber: insoluble and soluble. Insoluble fiber aids digestion as it moves food quickly through the intestines and out of the body. This, in turn, may help prevent constipation, diverticulitis (large intestinal wall weakens and balloons out), and colon cancer. Insoluble fiber is found in wheat bran, whole wheat, and most other whole grains, potatoes, and most other fruits and vegetables.

Soluble fiber can lower blood cholesterol and help manage blood sugar level. It also aids in digestion. This type of fiber is found in oat bran (outer coating of grain), dried beans, and fruit. Soluble fiber, like any cholesterol-lowering agent, is effective only when combined with a low-fat and low-cholesterol diet.

The average person consumes only half of the 30 grams of fiber recommended by the National Cancer Institute and other health organizations. Only a few food labels distinguish between the two types of fiber. Usually, they are lumped together under *dietary fiber.* With a well-balanced diet, including fruits, vegetables, oatmeal, and oat bran, you are likely to get the different types of fiber and all the benefits. See table 9.3 for the dietary fiber content of certain foods.

Table 9.3 Dietary Fiber Content of Selected Foods.

Vegetables	Serving size (*½ cup cooked unless otherwise marked)	Total fiber (grams)	Soluble fiber (grams)	Insoluble fiber (grams)
Peas	*	5.2	2.0	3.2
Parsnip	*	4.4	0.4	4.0
Potato	1 small	3.8	2.2	1.6
Broccoli	*	2.6	1.6	1.0
Zucchini	*	2.5	1.1	1.4
Squash, summer	*	2.3	1.1	1.2
Carrot	*	2.2	1.5	0.7
Tomato	*	2.0	0.6	1.4
Brussels sprouts	*	1.8	0.7	1.1
Beans, string	*	1.7	0.6	1.1
Onion	*	1.6	0.8	0.8
Rutabaga	*	1.6	0.7	0.9
Beet	*	1.5	0.6	0.9
Kale greens	*	1.4	0.6	0.8
Turnip	*	1.3	0.6	0.7
Asparagus	*	1.2	0.3	0.9
Eggplant	*	1.2	0.7	0.5
Radishes	½ cup raw	1.2	0.3	0.9
Cauliflower	*	0.9	0.3	0.6
Beans, sprouted	*	0.9	0.3	0.6
Cucumber	½ cup raw	0.8	0.5	0.3
Lettuce	½ cup raw	0.5	0.2	0.3

Fruits	Serving size (raw)	Total fiber (grams)	Soluble fiber (grams)	Insoluble fiber (grams)
Apple	1 small	3.9	2.3	1.6
Blackberries	½ cup	3.7	0.7	3.0
Pear	1 small	2.5	0.6	1.9
Strawberries	¾ cup	2.4	0.9	1.5
Plums	2 med	2.3	1.3	1.0
Tangerine	1 med	1.8	1.4	0.4
Apricots	2 med	1.3	0.9	0.4
Banana	1 small	1.3	0.6	0.7
Grapefruit	½	1.3	0.9	0.4
Peach	1 med	1.0	0.5	0.5
Cherries	10	0.9	0.3	0.6
Pineapple	½ cup	0.8	0.2	0.6
Grapes	10	0.4	0.1	0.3

Table 9.3 Dietary Fiber Content of Selected Foods. (continued)

Breads, Cereals	Serving Size (*½ cup cooked unless otherwise indicated)	Total fiber (grams)	Soluble fiber (grams)	Insoluble fiber (grams)
Bran (100 percent) cereal#	*	10.0	0.3	9.7
Popcorn	3 cups	2.8	0.8	2.0
Rye bread#	1 slice	2.7	0.8	1.9
Whole-grain bread#	1 slice	2.7	0.08	2.6
Rye wafers#	3	2.3	0.06	2.2
Corn grits	*	1.9	0.6	1.3
Oats, whole	*	1.6	0.5	1.1
Graham crackers#	2	1.4	0.04	1.4
Brown rice	*	1.3	0	1.3
French bread#	1 slice	1.0	0.4	0.6
Dinner roll#	1	0.8	0.03	0.8
Egg noodles	*	0.8	.03	0.8
Spaghetti	*	0.8	.02	0.8
White bread#	1 slice	0.8	0.03	0.8
White rice	*	0.5	0	0.5
Legumes				
Kidney beans#	*	4.5	0.5	4.0
White beans#	*	4.2	0.4	3.8
Pinto beans	*	3.0	0.3	2.7
Lima beans	*	1.4	0.2	1.2
Nuts				
Almonds	10	1.0		
Peanuts	10	1.0		
Walnuts, black	1 tsp. chopped	0.6		
Pecans	2	0.5		

Currently, researchers use different methods to analyze dietary fiber content in foods. Until a single testing protocol is adopted, precise fiber totals will vary from laboratory to laboratory.

Meats, milk products, eggs, and fats and oils are not listed in this food-fiber survey because they are virtually devoid of fiber content.

This symbol, (#), indicates that the fiber analysis was carried out on cooked food, rather than raw food.
Source: Reprinted by permission of *Nutrition Action Healthletter,* published by the Center for Science in the Public Interest.

Eating a Balanced Diet

The best way to receive adequate amounts of nutrients for proper health is to eat a balanced diet. This means including selections from the four basic food groups: milk and dairy products, protein-rich foods, fruits and vegetables, and bread and cereals.

Developed by the U.S. Department of Agriculture, the basic four food groups serve as a general food guide for planning a well-balanced diet. Although it has limitations, it provides a simple, practical guide for general meal planning and can be used to evaluate your overall food intake pattern.

It is based on the Recommended Dietary Allowances (RDAs) established by the National Academy of Sciences–National Research Council. The RDAs are reviewed for possible revision every five years. They are estimates of the optimal quantity of each nutrient required.

The Basic Food Groups

The following discussion will highlight the nutritional benefits of each food group and will identify the recommended daily adult serving minimums.

Grain Products

Grain products (breads and cereals) provide B-complex vitamins and energy to our diet. Four daily servings of any enriched or whole-grain bread or cereal are recommended. Foods in this group include noodles, rice, spaghetti, pancakes, tortillas, muffins, popcorn, cooked cereal, and boxed breakfast cereals.

Fruits and Vegetables

The fruits and vegetables group provides vitamin A, vitamin C, and fiber in our diets. Foods include citrus fruits, dark green vegetables, yellow and orange vegetables, fruit juices, canned or cooked vegetables and tossed salads. Consume at least one serving high in vitamin C daily, and at least one serving of a dark green, yellow, or orange vegetable containing fat-soluble vitamin A every other day. The adult recommendation is four daily servings.

Protein-rich foods

This food group provides our daily needs for protein, iron, and the B vitamins. Meats include all red meats (beef, pork, and game), fish, and poultry. Alternatives for meat include eggs, cheese, legumes (beans and dried peas), and peanut butter. The adult recommendation is 4 ounces maximum per day, preferably in two or more servings.

Dairy Products

The dairy products group provides high-quality protein and calcium. Whole milk, low-fat milk, skim milk, dried milk, yogurt, cheeses, and ice cream are foods included in this group. The adult recommendation is two cups of milk or two equivalent servings daily.

High-fat milk products contain more cholesterol, saturated fats, and additional calories than most people need. Low-fat milk products serve as healthy alternatives.

Junk Food

Where do soft drinks, cookies, candy, corn chips, potato chips, and pastries fit in? The junk food group is a good name because most do not fit into any of the other groups. Generally, junk foods provide additional calories along with significant amounts of sugar, salt, and fats. Junk foods are those highly processed foods that are typically high in calories and low in nutrients.

Fast Foods

Fast foods have become a way of life for many Americans. In contrast to junk food, the nutritional value of fast foods can vary greatly. Breakfast foods, potatoes, whole wheat breads, salad bars, low-fat meat and milk products, low-calorie foods, and vegetable oils are examples of how fast foods companies have expanded their offerings and made foods more nutritious. Many fast-food chains now provide nutritional information for their customers. Although fast foods can be nutritious, it would be unhealthy and expensive to rely on these foods as your main source of nutrition. Moderation is the key.

Nutrition Labeling

Reading the label is the best way to determine what nutrients are in processed or packaged food. Nutrition labeling is required for any enriched food with additional nutrients, or food that makes a specific nutritional claim. Enrichment refers to the replacement of nutrients lost in processing or the addition of nutrients not originally present.

A list of ingredients is usually included on the labels of packaged and processed foods. Ingredients are ranked by weight, with the item weighing the most listed first and the item weighing the least listed last. Although amounts of ingredients are not included, the ranking order can be helpful.

Healthy Nutrition

The U.S. Department of Agriculture and the Department of Health and Human Services have established seven dietary guidelines on the kinds of foods healthy Americans should be eating. The dietary guidelines do not promise good health.

Besides, people vary widely in their food needs. These general guidelines can help you evaluate your eating pattern and move toward positive changes. The seven dietary guidelines are:

1. Eat a variety of foods.
2. Maintain an ideal body weight.
3. Avoid too much fat, saturated fat, and cholesterol in your diet.
4. Eat foods with adequate starch and fiber.
5. Avoid too much sugar.
6. Avoid too much sodium.
7. If you drink alcohol, do so in moderation.

Proper nutrition is a worthwhile goal. Good food patterns based on variety, moderation, RDAs, and recommended servings from the four basic food groups build strong, healthy bodies. Eating well is essential to good health and contributes to quality of life and prevention of disease.

Weight Loss

10

Although few want it, millions have it—too much body fat. Americans consume more fat and sugar than any other country in the world. As a result, there are 60 to 70 million adults and 10 to 12 million school-age children in the United States who are too fat.

How Much Is Too Much Body Fat?

Many people use height and weight charts to determine what they should weigh, but the charts generally represent population averages, not ideal body weight. As the population becomes fatter, the averages on height and weight charts increase.

A second problem with height and weight charts is that being overweight does not seem to be a health problem as long as the extra weight is lean body tissue, or muscle. Therefore, it is quite possible for a muscular individual to be overweight, but healthy. It is not overweight but overfat that is a health problem.

A third problem concerns the normal weight and underweight individual. Although this person is considered within or below their normal weight range, he or she may have too much body fat and be unhealthy. Height and weight charts do not detect levels of body fat.

A height and weight chart can provide you with some information about how you compare to population averages. It can also give a general idea about whether or not you have accumulated too much body weight. Medical professionals often use 20 percent above ideal weight as an indicator of obesity. However, this method is not as accurate as measuring percent body fat, which is the percentage of total body weight that is stored body fat.

An overfat condition simply means your body is composed of too much fat. Obesity refers to a condition in which an excessive amount of body fat has been stored. There is a lack of accurate data regarding the level at which stored body fat becomes a serious health problem. However, there seems to be general agreement that men who are over 25 percent body fat and women who are over 30 percent body fat should be considered obese. See table 10.1 for standards of percent body fat.

Table 10.1   Percent Body Fat Chart.

	Men	Women
Too Much	More than 25 percent	More than 30 percent
Just Right	10–15 percent	15–20 percent
Too Little	Less than 5 percent	Less than 10 percent

Why Control Body Fat?

In the United States there are many physical, social, and psychological problems associated with having too much body fat. Some Americans are obsessed with being thin. At other times and in other cultures, overfatness was a social advantage, a sign of prosperity and health. This is not true in America today. Thin is in. The fashion world contends that to be attractive, people must be slim. More important than fashion, health is a concern with too much fat.

There are many physical reasons for not allowing yourself to become obese. Obesity is associated with several heart disease risk factors including high blood pressure, high cholesterol, and diabetes. Other health problems exist if the obese individual is lucky enough not to develop heart disease. Strokes or kidney problems may result due to high blood pressure. Blindness, heart attacks, strokes, and fat-clogged arteries can occur in an obese individual with diabetes. Obesity has also been associated with certain cancers, such as breast cancer for women and prostate and colon cancer for men. The obese may also suffer from degenerative joint diseases such as arthritis.

Besides frequent and serious illnesses, obesity has been linked to a shorter life span. Some research has indicated that those who are moderately overfat may have a 40 percent higher than normal risk of having a shortened life span. Obesity may result in a 70 percent higher than normal risk of having a shortened life span.

In America, there is a social stigma attached to being fat. The overfat are seen as unattractive, inadequate, unhealthy, undisciplined, insecure, depressed, having poor personalities, having higher anxiety levels, and having a lower self-concept than normal weight people. These characteristics are certainly not true of everyone who is overfat. However, those who find themselves with too much fat are still perceived this way.

As a result of social conditioning, the overfat often encounter teasing, ridicule, and rejection. In turn, psychological problems may result in the form of a poor body image, a sense of failure, a passive approach to life situations, and an expectation of rejection.

What Causes This Overfat Condition?

The most common cause of obesity is taking in more calories than are used up. The human body is very good at storing these excess calories in the form of body fat. The United States has developed the ability to produce an abundance of food. Meanwhile, modern technology has developed many new labor-saving devices. The net result is that the physical effort of daily life has decreased while the availability of food has been increased. For millions of Americans this has led to the accumulation of too much body fat.

Until recently, obesity was thought to be caused by overeating. However, recent evidence suggests that a lack of physical activity is more often the culprit. It has been found that the overfat do not necessarily eat more than their normal weight counterparts—they are less active.

In a few rare cases, glandular malfunction or some other medical problem may be the cause of obesity. However, for the vast majority of Americans, the problem is more calories are taken in than are being used up on a regular basis.

Obesity does not occur overnight. Creeping obesity is a term given to the gradual accumulation of stored body fat. For the average American, there is a gradual decrease in physical activity beginning in the late teens or early twenties. During this decline, eating habits tend to remain constant. It is not hard to see that if you continue to take in the same amount of calories, and use less of them, the excess will be stored as body fat. As a result of this pattern, the average adult American gains about one pound a year. This is not an alarming amount of weight until you figure that by age fifty, it will add up to about thirty pounds of excess body fat.

Along with a decrease in activity, there is a gradual loss of muscle tissue. Less muscle tissue combined with the gradual accumulation of stored body fat results in a rather rapid change in percent body fat. In addition, resting metabolic rate (calories needed at rest) also decreases with age. This decrease may be related to the loss of muscle tissue due to inactivity or it may be a natural occurence during the aging process. At any rate, if you maintain your same eating habits as you get older and decrease your level of physical activity, you are almost certain to accumulate body fat.

This problem is not limited to adults. If children take in more calories than they use up on a regular basis they also become obese. A very high percentage of obese children and adolescents become obese adults.

How Can Body Fat Be Measured?

Although body fat cannot be measured with absolute accuracy, there are several methods of estimating body fat that have proven to be fairly reliable and reasonably accurate. Methods for estimating percent body fat include underwater weighing, water displacement, X ray, ultrasound, electrical impedance, body girth, and skinfold measurement. Of these, skinfold measurement is one of the least expensive, most accurate, and most available methods.

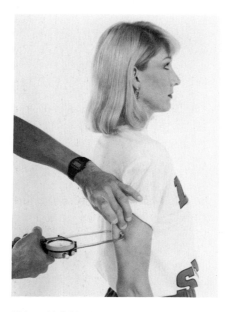

Using skinfold calipers to measure triceps skinfold.

About 50 percent of body fat is stored just beneath the skin. Skinfold calipers are used to measure the thickness of a fold of skin and the fat located directly under it. Taken at different body sites, the thickness of the skinfolds can be used to obtain a good estimate of total body fatness.

Activity 10a

The purpose of this activity is to estimate your percent body fat using skinfold caliper measurements.

Guidelines for Making Skinfold Measurements

1. All of the skinfold measurements should be made on the right side of the body.
2. The skinfold should be picked up between the thumb and index finger.
3. Measure the thickness of the skinfold approximately one centimeter from the fingers and at a depth that is equal to the thickness of the fold.
4. Make three measurements at each skinfold site. Use the average of the three measurements as the skinfold thickness for that site.
5. Release and regrasp the skinfold for each measurement.
6. Measurements made by two different people may vary slightly. If you are measured a second time, have the measurements made by the same person at the same time of day.

Skinfold Sites

To determine percent body fat for women use the sum of the skinfold measurements at the tricep, iliac crest, and thigh.

To determine percent body fat for men use the sum of the skinfold measurements at the chest, abdomen, and thigh.

Triceps Skinfold—Locate a point on the back of the upper arm halfway between the top of the shoulder and the tip of the elbow. Measure a vertical skinfold.

Iliac Crest—Locate a point on the side of the waist above the crest of the hip bone and slightly toward the front of the body, where there is a natural diagonal skinfold.

Thigh—Locate a point on the front of the thigh halfway between the hip joint and the knee joint. Measure a vertical skinfold.

Chest—Locate a diagonal fold halfway between the front of the armpit and the man's nipple.

Abdomen—Locate a point one inch to the right of the umbilicus and measure a vertical skinfold.

Use of the Nomogram

Add your three skinfold measurements (in mm) and mark this sum on the appropriate line of the nomogram (see figure 10.1). Place your age on the nomogram. Use a straight edge to connect these two points. Mark the place where the straight edge crosses the correct percent body fat line for your sex. What is your percent body fat?

What Can You Do about Excess Body Fat?

The energy-balance equation states that for your weight to remain constant, you must use up as many calories as you take in. When the amounts are not balanced, your weight changes. There are approximately 3,500 calories in one pound of stored body fat. If you take in an extra 500 calories a day, you will gain about one pound of body fat every seven days. Of course, the opposite is also true. If you take in 500 calories per day less than you need, you will lose about one pound every seven days.

The healthiest and most effective way to lose body fat is to combine a well-balanced diet with regular, moderate exercise.

A well-balanced diet is your source of dynamic energy. It should consist of foods high in nutrients that are prepared nutritiously. Your diet must provide all of the calories necessary to meet your energy needs. It must also include all of the nutrients necessary for healthy maintenance of your body. If essential nutrients are missing, your body cannot continue to function properly.

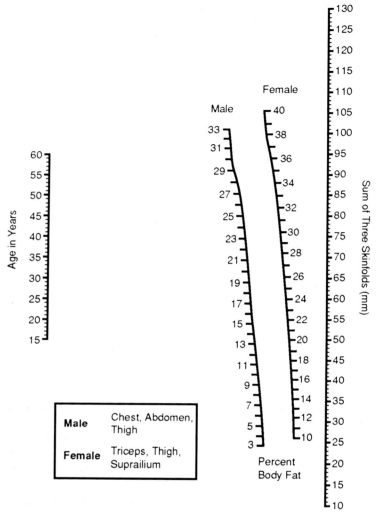

Baun, W. B., Baun, M. R., & Raven, P. B., 1981. A nomogram for the estimate of percent body fat from generalized equations. *Research Quarterly for Exercise and Sport*, 52:380–84.

Figure 10.1
Nomogram.

Exercise helps burn up calories. Because muscle contraction requires energy, the more your muscles contract, the more calories you will use. Experts are in agreement that exercise plays a key role in reducing the loss of lean body weight (muscle) and promoting fat loss. Dieting can cause up to 40 percent of your weight loss to be from protein and muscle. You want to lose fat, not muscle. The failure rate of dieting by itself is high. Therefore, exercise should be included in a weight-management program.

Table 10.2 The Caloric Cost of Walking (calories/miles)*

Walking Pace (mph)	Body Weight				
	100 lbs.	125 lbs.	150 lbs. 175 lbs.		200 lbs.
			Calories Burned		
3.0	52	66	79	92	105
3.5	54	67	80	94	107
4.0	58	72	87	101	116
4.5	65	81	97	113	129

*Based on Bubb et al., 1985. *Journal of Cardiac Rehabilitation* 5:462–65, 1985.

Fitness Walking and Fat Loss

Fitness walking makes five major contributions to your weight management program: it increases caloric expenditure, controls appetite, helps maintain resting metabolic rate, burns fat while increasing muscle mass, and helps reduce stress and tension.

Fitness walking burns up a lot of calories. Like other aerobic activities, it uses the large muscle groups of your body in repeated contractions for a relatively long period of time. Fitness walking a mile burns about the same amount of calories as jogging a mile. Walking just takes you longer. See table 10.2 to discover how many calories you can use based on your walking pace and body weight.

Fitness walking should not increase your appetite. Animal and human studies have indicated that exercise of light to moderate intensity and duration does not increase appetite, and may even reduce appetite.

Fitness walking may help keep your resting metabolic rate up while dieting. It increases the number of calories you use during your walks, and keeps your metabolic rate elevated after your workout is finished. Thus, your body continues to burn calories at a faster pace for several hours afterward. This uses up more calories than you normally would at rest. An elevated metabolic rate also makes you feel alert and alive.

Fitness walking builds fat-burning cells (muscle) while it reduces the size of fat-storing cells. Based on research to date, it appears that you cannot reduce the number of fat cells in your body. However, you can shrink their size and reduce the percentage of your body weight that is stored body fat. Because fitness walking is not as exhausting as some other forms of exercise, it is possible to exercise longer and burn more total calories.

Finally, fitness walking helps reduce stress and tension. The temptation to cheat on a diet is greatest during times of stress and tension. After a stressful, unpleasant day it is normal to look for a pleasant experience. Many people find this pleasure in eating and drinking. Going for a walk removes idle snacking time and helps reduce stress and tension.

Tips for Body Fat Control

If weight control is more important to you than cardiovascular health, you might adjust your fitness walking program by decreasing the intensity, increasing the duration, and increasing the frequency. This could result in more total calories expended during exercise. However, it is recommended that you stick with the exercise guidelines in chapter 7. By following the guidelines, you can expect three major benefits from your fitness walking program: cardiovascular fitness, weight control, and stress reduction.

One of the keys to permanent weight loss and fat reduction is to take the weight off slowly. Gradually reducing excess body fat allows you to remain healthy and motivated. Develop a new, healthier life-style that you can maintain for the rest of your life.

If you try to remove excess body fat too quickly, you are more likely to experience illness or injury. When this occurs you will have to stop your program until you are well again.

Losing weight too quickly may also result in the yo-yo syndrome, which is a cycle of losing weight and regaining it. If the weight is lost quickly, by diet alone, as much as half of the weight loss can be lean body tissue or muscle. The weight that is regained is mostly fat. The more often weight is lost and regained, the more fat is accumulated. This cycle can also lead to a unique form of high blood pressure called dieter's hypertension.

You should not attempt to lose more than one or two pounds of fat per week. To lose one pound of fat per week you will need a caloric deficit of 500 calories a day. If you fitness walk two and one-half miles you will burn about 250 extra calories. If you give up one hamburger you will take in about 250 calories less. Neither of these should be extremely difficult. You need not starve yourself or totally exhaust yourself with exercise if you combine diet and exercise.

During the first six to eight weeks of your exercise program, you may not lose any weight. Because muscle is more dense than fat, you may actually experience a slight increase in body weight during this time period. However, because the weight gained is muscle and the weight lost is fat, there should be a decrease in body circumference measurements. Beginning exercisers will often lose inches while remaining at the same body weight.

If you believe you need to lose a considerable amount of weight, be smart and safe–check with your physician. Your doctor should be able to tell if it is safe for you to combine a caloric reduction diet with a fitness walking program. Your physician may refer you to a dietician for an individualized diet plan.

Spot Reduction

A common misconception about exercise is spot reduction, which is the idea that to lose fat from a specific body part you need to exercise that body part. Examples of the spot reduction idea include sit ups to remove fat from the abdominal area and side bends to lose fat from the side of your waist. Research indicates that spot reduction does not work.

These specific exercises will develop the muscle tissue under the stored body fat and increase the strength or muscle endurance of the muscle tissue. However, unless there is a total caloric deficit created in the body, it appears that none of the energy will be taken from stored body fat. Even if a caloric deficit exists in the body, there is no evidence to indicate that a muscle can get energy from the nearest body fat storage area.

Guidelines for Fat Loss

Diet

Well-Balanced Diet

Food Groups	Recommended Daily Servings
Grain Products	4
Fruits and Vegetables	4
Dairy Products	2
Meat	2
Junk Food	0

Amount
Maintain recommended daily servings.
Eat smaller servings.
Not below 1,200 daily calories (women).
Not below 1,500 daily calories (men).

Exercise

Type	— Aerobic
Intensity	— 60–90% of maximum heart rate
Duration	— 30–60 minutes per session
Frequency	— 5–7 days per week

Mental Benefits

11

Although most people are aware of the physical health benefits, they may not be aware of the mental health benefits of fitness walking. Many regular fitness walkers believe the mental benefits are just as important, if not more important, than the physical benefits.

Your mind and body can only be separated in theory, for the purpose of study and discussion. In reality, the human body is one totally integrated organism that cannot be separated into component parts. Anything that affects your mind affects your body, and anything that affects your body affects your mind. An example of this mind-body relationship would be a stomach ulcer that has resulted from constant worrying.

Stress Reduction

Your mental and physical health are affected by your ability to manage stress. Medical doctors have estimated that as much as 70 percent of all illness may be stress related. Too much stress (distress) can lead to high blood pressure, heart disease, depression, schizophrenia, indigestion, increased cholesterol concentration, low back pain, headaches, cancer, and lower resistance to disease. Too little stress is also harmful. It can lead to boredom, loneliness, and suicide.

Humans adapt best to moderate stress. This is positive, enhancing stress that helps overcome laziness and provides the drive to be productive and excel. There is a relative stress level that is different for each individual. Your own moderate stress level should be located somewhere between having too much to do and being bored. It is a feeling of well-being that promotes optimal performance and efficiency.

One healthy coping strategy for dealing with excess stress is regular exercise. Fitness walking helps release the muscular tension that accumulates when you are under stress by alternately and rhythmically contracting and relaxing your muscles. This action pumps fresh blood and oxygen to all the living cells of your body. It also carries away the accumulated chemical waste products of stressful muscular tension, leaving you with a wonderful feeling of being refreshed and alive.

Fitness walking provides an opportunity to take a minivacation from the pressures of everyday life. It is a time to be by yourself, or with others, depending on which is most relaxing for you. Many regular walkers report that their fitness walking programs help them deal with their concerns of life, relationships, expectations of others, and money problems. As a stress management technique, fitness walking ranks high as an excellent lifelong activity for relieving stress.

```
┌─────────────────────────────────────────────────┐
│                                                 │
│                                                 │
│                 Too Much stress                 │
│                  (Overload)                     │
│                                                 │
│                                                 │
├─────────────────────────────────────────────────┤
│                                                 │
│                                                 │
│                                                 │
│                                                 │
│                                                 │
│                Moderate Stress                  │
│                 (Just Right)                    │
│                                                 │
│                                                 │
│                                                 │
│                                                 │
│                                                 │
├─────────────────────────────────────────────────┤
│                                                 │
│                                                 │
│                                                 │
│                Too Little Stress                │
│                  (Boredom)                      │
│                                                 │
│                                                 │
└─────────────────────────────────────────────────┘
```

Figure 11.1
The Stress Chart.

Positive Self-Esteem

The need for self-esteem includes a feeling of personal worth, success, achievement, self-respect, and self-confidence. To build self-esteem, it is important to be good in a specific area. This area should reflect your own interests, abilities, and opportunities.

Success breeds success. The feelings you gain by satisfying your need for self-esteem are apt to promote other achievements that will further encourage self-esteem.

A fitness walking program can help build self-esteem. It helps develop self-discipline, which can lead to a sense of accomplishment and a feeling of personal worth. Every fitness walking workout is a victory over laziness and low self-respect. The positive physical development that occurs as a result of a regular walking program can also contribute to an increase in self-confidence.

Believe in yourself and your abilities. Recognize your limitations and expect to grow from them. People who feel good about themselves regard their own opinions and decisions as worthwhile.

Fitness walking, along with good nutrition and adequate rest, can help you accomplish your goals in life. The more success you have, the more positive your self-esteem will be.

Improved Creativity and Problem-Solving Ability

A mental training program can be combined with your fitness walking program to help you become a creative thinker. This, in turn, can help you become a better problem solver. As an exercise, fitness walking promotes an increase in the oxygen supply to the brain. This can result in improved thinking ability, better memory, longer concentration, and heightened clarity of thought.

Some experts believe you can train yourself to think more creatively. As a result, you will be a better problem solver. To begin with, change your perspective. See things from a different point of view or a different angle. If you normally walk the same course every day, try walking in the opposite direction or walk somewhere else. If you normally walk in the evening, try a walk in the morning. If it rains, try a walk in the rain. You will often see things you have never seen before when you come at them from another direction or in different weather conditions.

Mental exercises like these, combined with your fitness walking program, can help you to overcome obstacles that block your imagination. By working your "imagination muscle" while you walk, you can add creativity and originality to your thinking.

Once you begin to see things from another point of view, you will be able to find new solutions to old problems. More options become available. You may even learn to view your work, play, and relationships with others differently.

Relief of Anxiety and Depression

There is still considerable discussion about the antidepressant effects of exercise. In part, the opportunity to set realistic goals and achieve them is important for the anxious or depressed individual. Fitness walking provides an opportunity to set these realistic goals and achieve them.

Sticking with a walking program develops self-control. Once self-control is established in one area, it can be applied to other areas. Gaining self-control through fitness walking can be used to replace negative behaviors (smoking, overeating, alcohol and drug abuse) that often contribute to anxiety and depression. Replacing negative behaviors with positive behaviors (fitness walking, good nutrition) can lead to a feeling of accomplishment and improved overall health.

Many mental health professionals now recommend walking for their anxious or depressed clients. They are encouraging their clients to get outdoors, open up their senses, and appreciate nature, instead of sitting at home feeling closed in, anxious, and depressed. In addition, many mental health professionals are now walking with their clients during therapy sessions. This helps clients open up and deal better with their concerns.

Depending on the severity of the anxiety or depression, fitness walking can help people get outside of themselves and away from a constant internal focus on their own problems. As their physical health improves, many depressed people stop feeling sorry for themselves. They begin to count their blessings and see what is good about their lives.

Two major steps in overcoming anxiety and minor depression are being more relaxed and feeling content. Many physicians believe that exercise is nature's best physical tranquilizer. A regular program of fitness walking can serve as one strategy to help relieve some types of emotional anxiety and control minor depression.

Increased Sense of Well-Being

A regular fitness walking program can increase the brain's supply of endorphins. Endorphins are naturally secreted hormones that act as the body's natural opiates. They are morphinelike substances that work in your brain to lower the sensation of pain and provide a sense of well-being. Research studies have shown that regular exercise increases the flow of endorphins to your brain and keeps them there longer. The moderate amount of endorphins released during fitness walking produces a feeling of being refreshed and energized. This leads to a positive exercise addiction. Those who are regular exercisers often say exercise makes them feel good.

Improved Sleeping Habits

Do you often lie awake at night with your mind racing, wishing you could fall asleep? Do you wake up in the morning feeling as if you haven't slept at all? A regular fitness walking program can contribute to a reduction in mental and physical tension. This can help you get to sleep more easily and sleep more soundly.

Better Quality of Life

A consistent and lifelong exercise program such as fitness walking will increase your ability to enjoy your leisure time. In addition, your productivity should improve, leading to more hours of satisfaction. Having more energy and enthusiasm will also lead to new opportunities. Others will begin to notice the "glow" radiating from you when you are in excellent physical condition and optimal health. Feeling good about yourself, learning to enjoy every day, and improving the quality of your life may be the ultimate benefits of a fitness walking program.

Sticking with It

12

The most difficult part of an exercise program is sticking with it. Research and experience indicate that people need more than knowledge or fear to stick with an exercise program.

Most adults in the United States know that a moderate amount of exercise on a regular basis would improve their health. Why then, do so many Americans still not exercise? Some American adults have had their physician tell them they must begin a regular exercise program or they will die prematurely. Yet, they still do not exercise.

Cardiac rehabilitation exercise programs for heart attack survivors have reported that only about 50 percent of these individuals will stick with an exercise program. This high dropout rate exists even though they realize an exercise program will reduce their risk of another heart attack. Clearly, knowledge and fear are not strong enough motivators for exercise adherence.

Although walking has a better adherence rate than many other exercise programs, the dropout range is still too high, around 25 to 50 percent. This means that one or two people out of every four who begin a fitness walking program will quit. Will you be one who quits? Or will you be one who has what it takes to make a commitment and stick with it?

What is your health worth? Do you believe you can buy it back with money after you have lost it? Keeping healthy isn't just luck. Adopting and maintaining a regular exercise program is one way to invest in a lifetime of good health.

Motivation

The most important psychological obstacle to regular exercise is lack of motivation. Being self-motivated is strongly related to sticking with your fitness walking program. One important question to ask yourself is "Do you believe your daily activities have an impact on your health?" If you answered yes, you are more likely to feel you have control over your own health.

Being healthy, physically fit, and attractive will help you gain more personal control over your life. Beginning a fitness walking program can be an important first step toward taking this control. People who demonstrate control over their lives tend to be happier. In fact, high-control people are twice as likely to say they are happy as low-control people.

Many people start exercise programs every year. Why do some stick with it while others drop out? One answer is motivation. Those who are highly motivated will stick with their exercise program. They will not allow any obstacles to interfere with their workouts. Those who are not motivated will look for reasons to skip an exercise session and drop out.

There are many motivational strategies that have proven to be successful for exercise adherence. What works for one person may not work for another person. If you are highly motivated to exercise for your health, you will find several strategies that work best for you.

Motivational Strategies

Set Clear and Definite Goals

Goal setting can give you direction and motivation. What do you want to achieve as a result of participation in a fitness walking program? If you have a burning desire to reach a goal you will be motivated.

To be effective your goals must be realistic. An example of an unrealistic goal would be to lose thirty pounds of body fat in two weeks. A realistic goal is one that you sincerely believe you can achieve. It may be difficult, but it is believable. An example of a realistic goal might be to lose one or two pounds of body fat each week as a result of regular fitness walking and reducing caloric intake.

Set goals you believe you can achieve. When you achieve a goal you can always set another one. Because success breeds success, each time you achieve a goal you gain confidence in yourself and your ability to achieve the next goal.

The most powerful goals are measurable and clearly defined. "I want to get in shape" is a noble desire but not a very good goal. How will you know when you are "in shape"? A better goal might be "I will walk two miles in thirty minutes on (a specific date)." When you time your walk on that day, you will know if you have accomplished your goal. If you have, set another definite goal. If you have not, evaluate your exercise program, figure out why you did not reach your goal, and make the necessary changes in your exercise program.

An important step in the goal-setting process is writing your goals down. Written goals are much more powerful than unwritten ones and much less likely to get changed. By writing your goals down, you become more committed to achieving them. They also provide clear outcomes to strive for and a way to measure your progress.

Activity 12a

The purpose of this activity is to fill out a fitness walking contract that will reaffirm your commitment to reach the goals you have set for yourself.

Once you have clearly defined your goals, fill in the contract below.

I, _____ , will commit myself to being in better health by following a fitness walking program.

The specific health and fitness goals of my walking program are:

1.
2.
3.
4.
5.

Specific date(s) I expect to reach my goal(s) are:

Other important reasons why I have committed myself to a fitness walking program:

1.
2.
3.

Guidelines to follow that will help me to stay with my fitness walking program:

1.
2.
3.

Support people that will help me with my fitness walking program:

1.
2.
3.

When I reach my goals, I will reward myself by:

If I fall short of my goals, I will punish myself by:

SIGNATURE _____ DATE _____

WITNESS _____ WITNESS _____

Reward Yourself

Reward yourself when you reach one of your goals. Give yourself something special, something you really want. Of course, it should be a healthy reward such as a vacation, new walking shoes, new clothes, a new music tape, or just a pat on the back. Only you know what would be an appropriate reward for yourself.

For some people, it is difficult to look too far into the future. They want instant gratification or daily rewards after each workout. Before and during the exercise session, these secondary rewards can provide an incentive to walk. Looking forward to this special treat is motivation enough to begin and complete the walk. Examples include taking a refreshing shower, watching a favorite television show, or going out for the evening.

Maintain a Positive Attitude

Often the difference between success and failure is attitude. A positive attitude produces positive results. You can program your mind for success by believing in yourself. With a positive attitude, you will look forward to each exercise session and enjoy your fitness walking program. Each workout can provide another opportunity to have fun and improve your health.

Strive to maintain a positive attitude every day you walk. Enjoy each walk. Think pleasant thoughts. It takes at least twenty-one days for a new behavior to become a habit so the first month of your fitness walking program is critical.

If you allow your attitude toward fitness walking to become negative, or if it becomes something you have to do instead of something you want to do, you might be headed toward failure.

Fitness walking needs to become an important part of your regular schedule, just like eating and sleeping. Don't ever wonder if you will walk today, know when you will walk today. Build it into your regular schedule. Once you begin to experience the beneficial effects, fitness walking will become its own reward because it will make you feel much better.

Close your eyes and imagine yourself achieving your goals. Make use of the self-fulfilling prophecy. If you repeat something about yourself over and over, it becomes part of your identity and you feel obligated to live up to it. Write your own script for who you want to be and how you want to live. Tell yourself over and over "I will stick to my exercise program. I will stick to my exercise program. I will stick to my exercise program." This will soon become part of you and you will be more likely to stick to your walking program. Fitness walking provides a great opportunity to repeat your positive affirmations while you do something healthy.

Make Fitness Walking a Priority

Once you decide to include fitness walking in your life, make a commitment. Place a high priority on your fitness walking time. Don't allow anything to interfere with your scheduled exercise time.

Regularity is important to the success of an exercise program. Regular exercise will soon become a healthy habit just like brushing your teeth, eating well-balanced meals, and receiving an adequate amount of sleep.

If you do not place a high priority on your fitness walking time, you might be setting yourself up for failure. If you decide to exercise "whenever you have time," you will frequently find that you don't have time. Irregular exercise is not very beneficial and can be harmful. An unplanned, irregular exercise program will soon deteriorate into no exercise program at all.

Take responsibility for your own health and life. Be in charge. Decide what is most important. If you value your health, place a high priority on good health habits. To reach your goals you will need to put forth your best effort. Reaching worthwhile goals will require dedication, discipline, and persistence.

Activity 12b

The purpose of this activity is to help you set priorities and identify those things that are most important to you.

List the ten most important things in your life right now. After you have written them down, rank them from one to ten. Is your health or your appearance in the top ten? If one of them is in the top ten, and it is a primary reason for exercising, you are more likely to stick with your fitness walking program. If your health and your appearance are not important, you are more likely to be an infrequent walker and eventually a fitness walking dropout.

Create a Personal Balance Sheet

This motivational strategy involves weighing the advantages and disadvantages of participating in a fitness walking program. The advantages of fitness walking are located in chapters 2, 9, 10, 11, and 14. Whenever you are tempted to skip a walk, look at your list of advantages. This will provide the extra incentive to put on your fitness walking clothes and take the hardest step of all—the first one.

Activity 12c

The purpose of this activity is to create a personal balance sheet to weigh the advantages and disadvantages of participating in a fitness walking program.

Draw a vertical line down the center of a blank sheet of paper. At the top of the left side of the page write the word advantages. At the top of the right side of the page write the word disadvantages. On the left side of the paper list all of the benefits and advantages to be gained by regular participation in a fitness walking program. Refer to chapters 2, 9, 10, 11, and 14 if you need help remembering the advantages. When you have listed all of the advantages and benefits you can think of, go to the right side of the paper and list the disadvantages of participating in a fitness walking program.

Post this list where you will see it every day. This may provide additional motivation to continue your fitness walking program.

Planning

Many people are so busy doing, they don't have time to plan what it is they should be doing. Consequently, a great deal of their time is not spent wisely. Every individual has exactly twenty-four hours to spend each day. How well you spend your time depends on how well you plan and how well you follow your plan.

Good habits are vital to success. Planning is a good habit. Plan a daily schedule, write it down, and follow it. Be sure to include fitness walking in your daily plan. Set aside a specific time for walking.

Do It

One of the most common barriers to success is procrastination or putting things off. Instead of starting a fitness walking program next year, next month, next week, or tomorrow, start today. Do it now. Change to a healthier life-style right now.

Chart Your Progress

Keep a regular exercise log. Record each fitness walking session. This will provide an account of your progress. The visual feedback will give you motivation and a sense of accomplishment, which will help you stick with your fitness walking program.

Date	Pulse	Minutes	Miles	Comments

Figure 12.1
One example of a Progress Chart.

There are many ways to chart your progress. Find the level of record keeping that is right for you. Some people just like to put a check mark on a chart or a calendar. Others like to keep detailed records of the exact distance, the exact time, the exact exercise heart rate, and so on.

Charting your performance allows you to see your progress and determine how close you are to reaching your goals. It is rewarding to see the positive changes that take place as a result of regular fitness walking.

Walk with Others

Walking with others is a strong motivator. It turns fitness walking into a social activity that can make it more enjoyable. Walking with others provides you with companionship. The other person or people involved can also provide encouragement. You are more likely to stick with your fitness walking program when you know that someone is counting on you to be at a designated meeting place at a designated time.

Add Variety

Boredom is sometimes given as an excuse for quitting an exercise program. While the same routine every day appeals to some people, there are others who are easily bored with repetition. Variety is the answer. If you become bored with repetition, use your creativity to invent new ways of adding variety to your fitness walking program.

Explore new routes (parks, golf courses, hiking trails, beaches, new neighborhoods, etc.), find new exercise partners, use earphones to listen to the radio or tapes (be careful around traffic), walk backward, use different walking speeds, walk in the shallow end of a swimming pool or ocean, use hand weights, walk hills, walk stairs, walk to complete errands, park farther away, or enter walking events. These are only a few ideas. Use your creativity to invent other fun variations for your fitness walking program. Be alert to the signs of burnout and change your routine before it's too late.

Motivation tends to drop off during extreme weather. Alternatives during hot weather include walking when it is cooler—early morning or late evening. Alternatives during cold or wet weather include walking in malls, in indoor recreational facilities, and up and down stairwells.

Select a Pleasing Route

Safety should be your first consideration when selecting a place to walk. Traffic must always be taken into account. Beside traffic, there are areas in some cities that are never safe at any hour. Choose the safest and most attractive route that is available to you. Some suggestions are parks, country roads, nice neighborhoods, and golf courses.

Walking with others can provide motivation.

Cross Training

Cross training involves the use of other fitness activities to replace or be used as a supplement to your fitness walking program. Participating in other fitness activities can help prevent burnout by increasing variety. Cross training can also help you stay active and produce a more complete development.

With fitness walking as the primary exercise, you may choose to add other activities such as swimming, rowing, cross-country skiing, aerobic dancing, weight training, biking, tennis, racquetball, basketball, and jogging. Combining these activities will increase your cardiovascular fitness. In addition, they can contribute to muscular strength, muscular endurance, body composition, and flexibility. You should receive a motivational boost from this variety that will inspire you to maintain consistent fitness workouts.

Reducing Barriers to Exercise

Staying on a regular fitness walking program means not giving in to convenient excuses such as "I'm too tired," "It's too cold to walk," "It's too hot to walk," "I don't have time to walk," "It's too dark to walk," and so on.

The following tips are recommended for reducing some barriers to exercise:

Place your walking shoes by the door so you will not have to hunt for them.

Keep your walking clothes in the same convenient place so you can always find them quickly and easily.

Lay out your walking clothes the night before if you plan to walk in the morning. If you plan to walk later in the day, lay out your walking clothes in the morning to remind you.

Schedule your fitness walking early in the morning. Later in the day, your time to walk will be more likely to conflict with other activities, commitments, and priorities.

Use cue cards containing inspirational messages. Place them in strategic places, such as your bathroom mirror or your refrigerator door. The cue cards will assist you in programming your mind with positive statements. Examples of inspirational messages include "I am really looking forward to my walk today," "I am going to look great when I lose ten pounds," "It is going to feel wonderful to relieve the stress and tension."

Find out which motivational strategies work for you and use them to maintain your fitness walking habit.

Join a Club

Walking clubs are being formed throughout the United States. There may already be a walking club where you live. You may want to join an established walking club or form one of your own.

Walking clubs can offer classes to teach the benefits of fitness walking and guidelines for healthy walking programs. Members can help each other learn fitness walking techniques that will improve performance. They can also provide support and encouragement for each other. A walking club could set up an awards program to recognize the achievements of the members.

During periods of extreme weather such as long cold winters or long hot summers, the club may be able to gain access to an indoor facility or build one of their own. They might even conduct fund-raising projects for charities or arrange trips to special walking events.

Participate in Special Events

Organized walking events are becoming popular. The events have distances for all fitness levels. Being healthy and fun, striding events are being organized across the country. Instead of being competitive, these events are more like a parade.

In addition to the striding events, many five-kilometer (5K) and ten-kilometer (10K) race walking events are being held annually. The number of race walkers participating in these events is growing rapidly.

Setting challenging personal walking goals for yourself can provide additional motivation for your fitness walking program. For example, if you complete your first 5K in forty-five minutes you may decide to set a goal to complete your next 5K race in forty-three minutes. This may add more direction and meaning to each training session and keep you looking forward to participating in your fitness walking program.

Work for a Presidential Sports Award

A Presidential Sports Award is available for fitness walkers. The goal is to walk 125 miles in fifty days, which averages 2.5 miles a day. Once you reach a level where you are walking three miles a day, send off for the forms. When you complete all of the requirements, send the forms in and you will qualify for a patch, a medal, and a certificate. The address is:

Presidential Sports Award
P.O. Box 706
Old Chelsie Station
New York, N.Y. 10011

Evaluate and Modify

As the weeks, months, and years pass, change will occur. Your needs, interests, fitness level, living conditions, weather, and availability of exercise facilities will change. As these changes take place, you will need to periodically evaluate your fitness walking program to determine if it is still providing the correct amount of exercise. The key is to maintain a program that meets your current fitness needs and interests.

Motivational strategies play an important role in sticking with your fitness walking program. Experiment with the different ideas and find the ones that work best for you. Refer back to this chapter any time you need a dose of encouragement or a shot of motivation. Keep in mind the most important health and fitness benefits come from a regular and lifelong program.

Activity 12d

The purpose of this activity is to identify motivational strategies that will help you stick with your fitness walking program.

Place a check by all of the motivational strategies you believe will help you stick with your fitness walking program. Once you have selected these strategies, try each one. Then incorporate the strategies that work the best for you.

_____ Clear and Definite Goals
_____ Reward Yourself
_____ Positive Attitude
_____ Make Fitness Walking a Priority
_____ Create a Personal Balance Sheet
_____ Planning
_____ Do It
_____ Chart Your Progress
_____ Walking with Others
_____ Variety
_____ Select a Pleasing Route
_____ Cross Training
_____ Reducing Barriers to Exercise
_____ Belonging to a Club
_____ Participate in Special Events
_____ Presidential Sports Award
_____ Evaluate and Modify

Aging and Exercise

13

What Is Aging?

Aging refers to the process of growing older. In addition to the passing of time, people associate a gradual decline in physical functioning with the aging process. With aging there is a gradual loss of ability to adapt to the external environment, maintain a stable internal environment, repair damaged cells, replace damaged cells, and recover from exertion. Reaction time is slower, resistance to disease is not as great, physical working capacity is reduced, recovery from effort is slower, and the various body structures are not as resilient.

When Does Aging Begin?

Technically, aging begins the moment after fertilization occurs, long before birth. However, aging is usually thought of as the gradual loss of functional ability that occurs during the adult years. In this chapter the term *aging* will refer to the process that occurs after full growth and development has been reached during the late teens or early twenties.

What Is Human Physiology?

Human physiology is the science that studies how the human body and all of its various parts function.

What Is the Normal Pattern of Growth and Development for Humans?

Human life begins with a period of fairly rapid growth and improvement in physiological functioning until full physiological maturity is reached at an approximate age of eighteen to twenty-five years. This is generally followed by a gradual decline in functional ability during the adult years that is referred to as aging.

How Rapidly Does Aging Occur?

An average rate of aging for most human organ systems is about 1 percent per year after an approximate age of thirty. Of course there can be a great deal of individual variation from the average. Some individuals are fit and alert well into their nineties while others are incapacitated before they are sixty.

What Affects the Rate of Aging?

The primary factors that affect the rate of aging appear to be heredity and life-style. At this time the genetic component is beyond your control. However, you do have some control over your life-style. A healthy life-style tends to slow the loss of functional ability as you grow older while an unhealthy life-style can accelerate the aging process.

One example of an unhealthy life-style behavior would be excessive sun exposure, which accelerates aging of the skin. A second example would be cigarette smoking, which results in a rapid loss of lung capacity. A third example is a lack of regular exercise, which results in decreased physical working capacity.

It is even possible that exercise slows the actual rate of deterioration of some cells and tissues. However, this is very difficult to study and document scientifically.

What Causes Aging?

At the present time no one really knows for sure what it is that causes aging. There are several theories that attempt to explain the aging process. These theories can be grouped into two categories, damage theories and programmed aging theories.

The damage theories all describe different ways in which cells can become damaged with age and are not able to continue to function or adapt as well as they could at a younger age. Those cells that cannot divide to produce new identical cells after full maturity may be affected the most, specifically the nerve cells and muscle cells.

The programmed aging theories are based on the idea that cells are genetically programmed to age at a certain rate.

There is not any one theory of aging that is accepted by everyone. There are many changes that occur within the cell during the aging process. The difficulty is determining which of these changes are causing aging and which changes are a result of aging.

Which Organ Systems Are Affected Most During the Aging Process?

The functioning of some organ systems is easier to measure than others. The ones where aging has been noticed most are the cardiovascular system, the pulmonary system, the nervous system, the muscular system, and the skeletal system.

How Does Aging Affect Physical Performance?

The decrease in physical performance capacity generally parallels the decrease in circulatory capacity and the decrease in muscle mass. This decrease in physical performance is about 1 percent per year from ages twenty-five to sixty. After sixty performance appears to decrease at a rate of about 2 percent per year. Of course, this will vary from one individual to another and from one activity to another.

The greatest potential for sports performance occurs for most individuals between eighteen and thirty years of age. After that there is generally a decline in sports performance. During the last twenty years there has been a tremendous increase in the number of older adults participating in sports and activities. Some of these older adults are setting records in sports performances that were not considered possible just a few years ago.

The decline in sports performance is not nearly as great among those who continue to exercise on a regular basis as it is for those who are sedentary. A moderate amount of exercise on a regular basis keeps physiological functioning at a higher level throughout the adult years. This results in a higher quality of life for those individuals.

Research studies have reported that losses in physiological function are more closely related to activity level than to age.

Does Exercise and Sports Participation During Youth Provide Lifelong Protection Against Aging?

No, while activity during youth provides a good base to build from, it appears that exercise is only beneficial in your later adult years if you continue to exercise on a regular basis.

How Does Aging Affect the Cardiovascular System?

The cardiovascular system consists of the heart, the blood vessels, and the blood. With aging there is generally a decrease in maximum heart rate, stroke volume, and cardiac output. There is also a decrease in the diameter of the coronary arteries, which supply blood to the heart muscle. The resulting reduction in cardiac output (the amount of blood pumped per minute) averages about 1 percent per year.

How Does Exercise Affect the Cardiovascular System?

For those who participate in regular aerobic exercise there is an increase in stroke volume, cardiac output, and coronary artery diameter. Because of these increases the loss of circulatory capacity is only about half of that seen in the average individual who does not exercise.

Does Exercise Reduce the Risk Factors Associated with Cardiovascular Disease?

Yes, a moderate amount of regular aerobic exercise directly reduces the risk of cardiovascular disease. In addition, it also has a positive influence on these other risk factors: obesity, stress, high blood pressure, and blood fat concentrations.

How Does Aging Affect Lung Functioning?

With aging there is generally a gradual increase in stiffness and a loss of elasticity in the lung tissue and the chest wall. There is also a weakening of the muscles of respiration. As a result there is increased difficulty and decreased efficiency of breathing with aging.

There is a gradual reduction in vital capacity (the amount of air that can be moved in and out of the lungs) and a corresponding increase in residual volume (the amount of air that remains in the lungs after forced expiration).

How Does Exercise Affect Lung Functioning?

Exercise cannot repair damaged lung tissue but it can improve the functional capacity of the remaining tissue. In addition, middle-aged and older adults who continue endurance training do not lose the elasticity in the lung tissue and chest wall as quickly as sedentary individuals who are the same age.

What Is Oxygen Consumption?

Oxygen consumption is the ability to get oxygen from the surrounding air to all of the living cells inside the body.

How Does Aging Affect Oxygen Consumption?

Maximum oxygen consumption generally declines at a rate of about 1 percent per year after age thirty. This decrease in oxygen consumption is related to the decrease in maximum cardiac output.

How Does Exercise Affect Oxygen Consumption?

The loss of ability to take in oxygen from the surrounding air and deliver it to the cells is not as great among those who continue to participate in regular endurance exercise. This results in an increased quality of life for those who exercise. It is possible for a fit sixty-year-old to have a higher oxygen consumption capacity than an unfit twenty-year-old.

How Does Aging Affect the Muscular System?

During the aging process there is a loss of contractile elements, capacity for force production, fast twitch muscle fibers, strength, power, high speed movement, oxidative enzymes, glycolytic enzymes, size of mitochondria, number of mitochondria, physical working capacity, myosin, adenosine triphosphate (ATP), ATPase, and creatin phosphate. These changes are accompanied by increases in the percentage of slow twitch fibers, the nervous impulse needed to cause muscle contraction, and the recovery time necessary between muscle contractions. All of this adds up to an average loss of strength of about 10 to 20 percent from ages twenty-five to sixty. How much of this loss is due to natural biological aging and how much is due to a lack of exercise?

One research study that was conducted in a machine shop found no significant difference in handgrip strength in men ranging in age from twenty-two to sixty-two years old. Perhaps the loss of strength with aging is more closely related to lack of exercise than to age.

How Do Older Adults Respond to Strength Training?

On the same training program older adults demonstrated the same rate of strength gain when it was expressed as a percentage of their starting strength level. The younger men generally started at a higher strength level and experienced a greater absolute strength gain. The younger men experienced more hypertrophy (increase in muscle size) while the older men increased their strength through higher activation levels. This lack of hypertrophy could be related to declining testosterone levels in the older men and might help account for the fact that women of all ages can experience great increases in strength with very little increase in muscle size.

What Is Metabolic Rate?

Metabolism is the total of all of the chemical changes taking place in the body. Metabolic rate refers to the rate at which these chemical changes are taking place.

How Does Aging Affect Metabolic Rate?

There is generally a decline in metabolic rate of approximately 3 percent every decade during the adult years. This decline in metabolic rate may parallel the loss of muscle tissue. If eating habits remain constant as you lose muscle tissue, and your resting metabolic rate slows down, the excess calories will be stored as body fat.

Because muscle tissue can use up calories at a high rate it is important to maintain your muscle tissue through regular exercise to help avoid gaining body fat.

What Is Body Composition?

Body composition refers to what the body is composed of. A particular concern is what percentage of the total body weight is stored body fat. This is important because an excessive amount of body fat is unhealthy.

How Is Body Composition Affected by Aging?

From the late teens to the sixties there is usually an increase in total body weight, total body fat, and the percentage of the total body weight that is stored body fat. The average sedentary individual maintains eating habits that were formed during the high metabolic years of youth while a decrease in activity level, muscle tissue, and resting metabolic rate occur. This results in a gradual accumulation of stored body fat.

For many children in the United States the accumulation of body fat begins very early. A very large percentage of obese children become obese adults.

Do Humans Lose Body Fat after Age Sixty?

Some research studies indicate such a loss but these must be interpreted with care. Many of the obese individuals may have died before age sixty so that the population measured may not include the same number of overfat individuals as the younger age groups. Also, there is a greater chance that this age group is losing weight as a result of some other disease condition.

Does Body Fat Affect the Length of Life?

Research studies with animals have shown that the ones that were kept at a lower but healthy body weight lived significantly longer than those who were overfat.

Life insurance companies have found that humans who have too much body fat have a significantly shorter life expectancy.

How Does Exercise Affect Back Pain?

Back pain is often a result of weak muscles and too much body fat. Strengthening the abdominal muscles and the back muscles, stretching the hip flexor and hamstring muscles, and losing excess body fat can significantly reduce or eliminate back pain for the majority of individuals.

Some studies have reported as much as an 80 percent success rate in reducing back pain with proper exercise.

How Does Aging Affect the Nervous System?

There is a gradual decline in the functioning of the nervous system with increasing age. This results in slower reaction time, slower movement time, decreased vision, hearing loss, decrease in short-term memory, and an inability to handle several different bits of information at one time.

Does Exercise Benefit the Central Nervous System?

Animal studies have indicated that regular exercise is beneficial to the maintenance of the central nervous system. This may be due to the high oxygen saturation level that is necessary in the brain.

It has also been observed that older adults who participate in regular endurance exercise seem to be more alert than the sedentary individuals who are the same age.

What Affect Does Aging Have on Bone Tissue?

With aging there is a decrease in bone density, bone strength, and bone mineral content. This bone demineralization is referred to as osteoporosis. Bone density is lost at a rate of about 1 percent per year after ages thirty to thirty-five in women and ages fifty to fifty-five in men.

What Affect Does Exercise Have on Bone Tissue?

A moderate amount of exercise on a regular basis results in an increase in bone density, bone strength, and bone mineral content.

How Does Aging Affect Joints?

With increasing age there is generally an increase in joint stiffness, a loss of flexibility, and a loss of mobility.

How Does Exercise Affect Joints?

Exercise generally increases flexibility and joint mobility while decreasing joint stiffness.

What Are Hypokinetic Diseases?

Hypokinetic diseases are those diseases that are caused or contributed to by a lack of physical activity. Examples are cardiovascular disease, back pain, obesity, high blood pressure, ulcers, some mental disorders, some forms of diabetes, insomnia, and depression.

What Effect Does Exercise Have on Hypokinetic Disease?

Some research has indicated that those who exercise regularly have a lower incidence of stroke, respiratory diseases, all cancers, and deaths from all causes.

Cardiovascular diseases are the leading cause of death in the United States. The risk of suffering from cardiovascular disease is lower for those who participate in endurance exercise on a regular basis.

Higher rates of colon cancer have been associated with low physical activity levels. Adult onset (type II) diabetes responds well to regular exercise. Some types of high blood pressure can be brought back down to a normal level with regular exercise.

Does Exercise Affect the Length of Life?

By improving physiological functioning and reducing the risk of premature death from a variety of hypokinetic diseases, exercise may actually extend the length of an individual's life. A moderate amount of exercise performed on a regular basis may help humans approach the ideal conditions necessary for the longest possible life.

Even if life is not one day longer because of exercise the increased vitality and mobility that is experienced by older adults who exercise greatly increases the enjoyment and quality of the adult years.

How Does Aging Affect the Ability to Respond to a Physical Training Program?

Older adults can increase their fitness level and improve their physical performance. The percentage improvement based on their starting level is about the same as it is for younger adults. However, older adults generally have slower recovery rates, start at a lower level, and have less capacity for adaptation.

It is wiser to be a healthy, physically fit, sixty-year-old than for a sixty-year-old to try to be eighteen again. The same is true for those in their thirties, forties, and fifties.

What Is Life Span?

Life span refers to the maximum length of time a person could live under ideal conditions. All life forms on this planet have a life cycle and a life span that is relative to their species. The maximum life span for humans is about 110 to 120 years. This has been relatively constant for the last 2,000 years.

The longest documented life in modern times was a Japanese man who lived 120 years 237 days. He died in February 1986. The longest documented life in the United States was a woman who lived 113 years.

What Is Life Expectancy?

Life expectancy refers to the number of years an individual might expect to live in a specific society under the existing conditions at that time. These living conditions are almost always less than ideal.

Has Life Expectancy Changed in the United States?

While life span has not changed, life expectancy has increased dramatically in the United States during this century. Life expectancy for men born in the United States in 1900 was forty-six years; for men born in the United States in 1990 life expectancy is seventy-one years. Life expectancy for women born in the United States in 1900 was forty-nine years; for women born in the United States in 1990 life expectancy is seventy-nine years.

Much of this increase can be accounted for by reduced infant mortality and advances in medical science that have eliminated many of the infectious diseases. More people are living longer. The United States is rapidly becoming a nation of older citizens. The absolute number of older people is increasing and the percentage of the population that is made up of older people is also increasing. One projection is that by the year 2,000 one-fourth of the people in the United States will be over sixty-five years of age.

What Is the Negative View of the Aging Process?

The person with a negative outlook on life might say that life is all downhill, ultimately ending in death. So why bother trying to do anything about it. These people generally do not enjoy life.

What Is the Positive View of the Aging Process?

The person with a positive outlook on life might say that every day people grow and change. Every day they have an opportunity to change in a positive direction and to grow in some positive way. These are generally the people who are enjoying life.

Can You Participate in Your Own Creation?

Humans have an opportunity to participate in their own creation. The process of creation does not end with birth but continues throughout life. Living cells have a functional time limit. All cells serve their function and eventually die. Millions of the cells in your body are replaced every day. In terms of living cells, you are not the exact same person you were last year, yesterday, or even an hour ago. You are in a continual process of changing, growing, becoming, and being created. What will you be like tomorrow, next week, or next year? Your attitude, behavior, and life-style choices have a significant impact on who and what you will become.

Healthy Life-Style

14

Many wise Americans are discovering the value of living a healthy life-style. There has been a significant increase in the number of people who desire a better quality of life. This increase is partly due to the findings of recent scientific studies. Evidence now indicates that positive life-style behaviors can have a significant influence on health, quality of life, and optimal well-being.

Living a quality life means becoming the best you can be and enjoying your life experience. It includes development in all areas of your life. One area is optimal health. With a high degree of health, you are more likely to achieve your fullest potential in other areas of life, including family, school, work, and leisure time.

Wellness is a popular term referring to optimal health. It includes a life-style that contributes to the achievement of the highest level of well-being. A central idea of wellness is that the adoption of health-enhancing behaviors will help reduce disease risk factors and lead to better health. Wellness encourages people to become more actively involved in their health by taking more personal responsibility.

The current health problems in the United States are quite different from those at the turn of the century. During the early 1900s the leading causes of death were infectious diseases such as pneumonia, influenza, and tuberculosis. At the present time, the leading causes of death in the United States are heart disease, cancer, strokes, and accidents. These causes of death are not infectious and cannot be spread from person to person. They are related to negative life-style behaviors such as smoking, poor nutrition, lack of exercise, obesity, chemical dependency, drinking and driving, and excessive stress.

Health

Health is a dynamic quality that changes constantly. It is a term describing your overall level of functioning at a particular point in time. Optimal health includes a high level of functioning often characterized by vitality, a zest for life, and being in harmony with nature and humanity.

Although you may be in good health most of the time, your health is not constant. You will still have times during which you suffer from a cold, the flu, allergies, or other health problems. However, maintaining a healthy life-style should keep these health problems and their duration to a minimum.

I have never felt better	Optimal Health (Wellness)
I feel great	Excellent Health
I feel good	Good Health
I feel fine	Above-Average Health
I feel OK	Neutral
I don't feel so good	Minor Illness
I feel rotten	Major Illness
I have never felt worse	Critical Illness
	Death

Figure 14.1
Wellness-Illness Continuum.

The Wellness-Disease Continuum

The wellness-illness continuum shows that wellness, or optimal health, is the highest level of functioning possible (see figure 14.1). All of the systems in your body are functioning perfectly. The other end of the continuum represents the complete loss of functioning, or death. Every living person is somewhere between these two extremes. Where are you? Which direction is your life-style taking you? Are you headed upward toward a healthier and more abundant life or downward toward suffering and premature death?

As you can see on the wellness-illness continuum, the absence of illness does not mean you are in good health. Your position on the continuum depends on your total health and is influenced by your degree of health in each of the following dimensions: physical, mental, emotional, social, environmental, psychological, spiritual, and vocational. The achievement of optimal health is related to the development of each of these areas.

Physical Health

Developing physical health includes being physically fit, eating a well-balanced diet with the recommended servings of nutritious foods, being free from chemical dependency, and getting adequate sleep and rest.

Mental Health

Developing mental health includes continuing to expand your knowledge, sharing your knowledge with others, and increasing your creativity.

Emotional Health

Developing emotional health includes experiencing a variety of emotions but controlling your responses, expressing your emotions appropriately and comfortably, and showing respect and affection for others.

Social Health

Developing social health encourages satisfying relationships with others and establishing a sense of belonging within your community.

Environmental Health

Developing environmental health includes the reduction of environmental health hazards at home, on the job, and in your community. This includes avoiding or reducing your exposure to radiation, toxic wastes, air pollution, water pollution, noise pollution, and overcrowding.

Psychological Health

Developing psychological health includes the development of your ability to deal with stress and your ability to solve problems.

Spiritual Health

Developing spiritual health includes a belief in and acceptance of some unifying and controlling force more powerful than any human. It embraces a faith and value system that is consistent with your beliefs about that force. Spiritual health also encourages living in harmony with your beliefs and values.

Vocational Health

Developing vocational health includes job satisfaction and working in harmony with others to accomplish something worthwhile.

To achieve wellness, some development of each of the eight dimensions of total health is necessary (see figure 14.2). There should also be some balance to this development. A moderate degree of health in all eight dimensions is more desirable than being strong in some and weak in others. Each area can contribute to your health and your enjoyment of life.

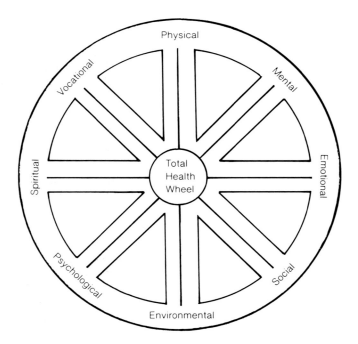

Figure 14.2
Total Health Wheel.

Activity 14a

The purpose of the total health wheel activity is to assess your current level of health in the eight dimensions.

Place a dot on each line of the total health wheel that best represents where you feel you are now. Dots placed close to the inner circle (hub) represent a lower level of health while dots placed near the outer circle (rim) indicate a higher level of health. Connect the dots. How balanced is your development? Are you close to achieving a high level of health in each dimension? What are your strengths? What are your weaknesses? What behaviors can you adopt, modify, or eliminate to improve your health?

A key in your efforts toward optimal health is to stay in touch with your feelings, attitudes, beliefs, and values. Only you can decide what combination of development in each dimension will make your life healthier and more enjoyable. Accept more personal responsibility for your health. You can do this by improving your shortcomings while maintaining your strengths.

Major Factors That Affect Your Health

Your total health depends on many factors. Some of these factors are under your direct control while others are not. An awareness of the factors that are not under your direct control may often help you deal more effectively with them. This is true even if you cannot directly control them. All of the factors are interrelated. They all influence each other as well as your total health.

Major factors that influence your health include: life-style behaviors, inherited biological characteristics, psychological environment, physical environment, medical care, accidents, injuries, and diseases.

Of all the major factors, life-style is currently the most important, and the one over which you have the most control. The choices you make today will lead toward good health or illness. The effects of these daily decisions are compounded over time. The accumulation of good choices will move you toward optimal health and a quality life. The accumulation of bad choices will move you toward suffering, disease, and premature death.

Making wise choices and adopting positive life-style habits will enhance your health status. If your life-style includes certain specific behaviors, your risk of disease will be lower and you may even live longer in good health. The following seven health practices were found to be highly related for promoting good health.

1. Not using tobacco, especially cigarette smoking.
2. Not drinking alcohol, or drinking only in moderation (no more than two drinks a day).
3. Eating breakfast every day.
4. No snacking between meals.
5. Maintaining a healthy body weight and a healthy level of body fat.
6. Sleeping seven to eight hours each night.
7. A moderate amount of exercise on a regular basis.

Fitness Walking and a Healthy Life-Style

Fitness walking is one positive behavior that can contribute to a healthy life-style. It is not a cure-all. It cannot solve all of your health problems. For you to develop to your full health potential and enjoy the benefits of a healthy life-style, fitness walking needs to be incorporated as one part of a much larger total health program. This larger program involves being aware of all the daily practices that have an impact on your health and modifying them in a positive direction.

One place to start is by reducing your risk of cardiovascular disease because it is the number one cause of death in the United States. Lower your risk of cardiovascular disease by following these recommendations: stop smoking, exercise regularly, change to a healthy diet, control blood pressure, and maintain a healthy body fat level.

Enjoy your walk through life.

Besides these changes, have a regular physical examination, a regular dental examination, practice regular self-examinations for breast cancer or testicular cancer, watch for signs of skin cancer, and follow safe sex practices. Also, practice relaxation strategies to reduce harmful stress, avoid smoke-filled environments, wear your seat belt every time you get in a moving vehicle, and don't drink and drive.

Congratulations are in order if you have started a fitness walking program. You have taken a first step toward improving your health. You should not attempt to make too many changes in your life-style at one time. Change is uncomfortable. If you try to make too many changes, and you become too uncomfortable, you are more likely to revert back to your old comfortable habits. This occurs even if you know your old habits are not good for you. Stick with your fitness walking program until it becomes a regular habit.

Once fitness walking becomes an integral part of your life, choose another health behavior to improve. As the years go by, maintain your strengths and work on your weaknesses. Because optimal health or wellness is an ideal that is probably never reached, there is always room for growth and development. Continue to walk your way toward better health. Remember to enjoy the journey every day on your walk through life.

Activity 14b

The purpose of this activity is to help you identify life-style behaviors that are enhancing or harming your health.

Place a check in either the positive or the negative column for each life-style behavior. Add up the positive and negative behaviors. Are you satisfied with your results? What are your healthy life-style behaviors? What are your unhealthy life-style behaviors? What are your plans to improve the life-style behaviors that are taking away from your health?

LIFE-STYLE BEHAVIOR	+	−
Tobacco use	—	—
Avoid smoke-filled environments	—	—
Alcohol consumption	—	—
Maintaining a healthy body weight	—	—
Maintaining a healthy percent body fat	—	—
Controlling blood pressure	—	—
Adequate sleep and rest	—	—
Regular moderate exercise	—	—
Practice stress-management techniques	—	—
Eating breakfast	—	—
Maintain a well-balanced diet	—	—
Limit salt intake	—	—
Limit sugar intake	—	—
Limit fat intake	—	—
Wear seat belts	—	—
Drinking and driving	—	—
Regular physical examination	—	—
Regular dental examination	—	—
Monthly self-exam for lumps or thickening of the skin	—	—
Practice safe sex	—	—
Attitude toward life	—	—
Use of drugs	—	—

References and Suggestions for Further Reading

Allsen, P. E. (1978). *Conditioning and physical fitness: Current answers to relevant questions.* Dubuque: Wm. C. Brown.

Allsen, P. E., Harrison, J. M., & Vance, B. (1984). *Fitness for life: An individualized approach* (3d ed.). Dubuque: Wm. C. Brown.

Alter, M. J. (1988). *Science of stretching.* Champaign, IL: Human Kinetics.

Althoff, S. A., Svoboda, M., & Girdano, D. A. (1988). *Choices in health and fitness for life.* Scottsdale, AZ: Gorsuch Scarisbrick.

Anderson, B. (1980). *Stretching.* Bolinas, CA: Shelter.

Bowerman, W. J., & Harris, W. E. (1967). *Jogging.* New York: Grosset & Dunlap.

Brooks, G. A., & Fahey, T. D. (1985). *Exercise physiology: Human bioenergetics and its applications.* New York: Macmillan.

Brooks, G. A., & Fahey, T. D. (1987). *Fundamentals of human performance.* New York: Macmillan.

Brown, H. L. (1986). *Lifetime fitness.* Scottsdale, AZ: Gorsuch Scarisbrick.

Bruess, C., & Richardson, G. (1989). *Decisions for health* (8th ed.). Dubuque: Wm. C. Brown.

Cairns, M. (1985). Racewalking—A fitness alternative. *Journal of Physical Education, Recreation, and Dance, 50*–51.

Campbell, K. R., Andres, R., Greer, N. L., Hintermeister, R., & Rippe, J. (1987). The effects of fatigue on selected biomechanical parameters in fitness walking. *Medicine and Science in Sports and Exercise, 19,* 518.

Coleman, R. J., Wilkie, S., Viscio, L., O'Hanley, S., Porcari, J., Kline, G., Keller, B., Hsieh, S., Freedson, P. S., & Rippe, J. (1987). Validation of a one-mile test for estimating VO2 max in 20–29 year olds. *Medicine and Science in Sports and Exercise, 19,* 528.

Cooper, K. H. (1968). *Aerobics.* New York: Bantam.

Cooper, K. H. (1970). *The new aerobics.* New York: Bantam.

Cooper, K. H. (1977). *The aerobic way.* New York: Bantam.

Cooper, K. H. (1982). *The aerobics program for total well-being: Exercise, diet, emotional balance.* New York: Bantam.

Cooper, M., & Cooper, K. H. (1972). *Aerobics for women.* New York: Bantam.

Corbin, C. B., & Lindsey, R. (1988). *Concepts of physical fitness with laboratories* (6th ed.). Dubuque: Wm. C. Brown.

Corbin, D. E. (1988). *Jogging.* Glenview, IL: Scott, Foresman.

Couey, R. B. (1982). *Building God's temple.* Minneapolis: Burgess.

DeBenedette, V. (1988). Keeping pace with the many forms of walking. *The Physician and Sportsmedicine, 16*(8), 145–150.

deVries, H. A. (1986). *Physiology of exercise: For physical education and athletics* (4th ed.). Dubuque: Wm. C. Brown.

DiGennaro, J. (1983). *The new fitness: Exercise for everybody.* Englewood, CO: Morton.

Dishman, R. K. (Ed.). (1988). *Exercise adherence: Its impact on public health.* Champaign, IL: Human Kinetics.

Ferrini, A. F., & Ferrini, R. L. (1989). *Health in the later years.* Dubuque: Wm. C. Brown.

Fixx, J. F. (1977). *The complete book of running.* New York: Random House.

Fox, E. L. (1984). *Sports physiology* (2d ed.). Philadelphia: Saunders.

Fox, E. L., Bowers, R. W., & Foss, M. L. (1988). *The physiological basis of physical education and athletics* (4th ed.). Philadelphia: Saunders.

Fox, E. L. & Mathews, D. K. (1981). *The physiological basis of physical education and athletics* (3d ed.). Philadelphia: Saunders.

Friedman, R. M. (Ed.). (1987). *Cholesterol testing: The numbers game.* New York: University of California, Berkeley, Wellness Letter.

Friedman, R. M. (Ed.). (1987). *Fish oil pills: Jumping the gun.* New York: University of California, Berkeley, Wellness Letter.

Friedman, R. M. (Ed.). (1989). *Cholesterol: The good, the bad, and the very confusing.* New York: University of California, Berkeley, Wellness Letter.

Friedman, R. M. (Ed.). (1989). *Your fiber IQ.* New York: University of California, Berkeley, Wellness Letter.

Getchell, B. (1983). *Physical fitness: A way of life* (3d ed.). New York: John Wiley & Sons.

Greer, N., Campbell, K., Andres, R., Hintermeister, R., & Rippe, J. (1987). An evaluation of walking and running shoes during walking. *Medicine and Science in Sports and Exercise, 19,* 517.

Greer, N. L., Campbell, K. R., Foley, P. M., Andres, R. O., & Rippe, J. M. (1986). An assessment of the reliability of ground reaction forces during walking. *Medicine and Science in Sports and Exercise, 18,* S81.

Hafen, B. Q., Thygerson, A. L., and Frandsen, K. J. (1988). *Behavioral guidelines for health and wellness.* Englewood: CO: Morton.

Hagerman, G. R., Atkins, J. W., McMurtry, J. G., & Steadman, J. R. (1987). *Efficiency walking and jogging.* New York: Bantam.

Health Information Library. (1986). *Nutrition: Better choices for wellness.* Daly City, CA: Krames Communications.

Henderson, J. (1988). *Total fitness: Training for life.* Dubuque: Wm. C. Brown.

Hesson, J. L. (1985). *Weight training for life.* Englewood, CO: Morton.

Hockey, R. V. (1985). *Physical fitness: The pathway to healthful living* (5th ed.). St. Louis: Times Mirror/Mosby.

Hoeger, W. W. K. (1986). *Lifetime physical fitness and wellness: A personalized program.* Englewood, CO: Morton.

Hoeger, W. W. K. (1988). *Principles and laboratories for physical fitness and wellness.* Englewood, CO: Morton.

Jonas, S., & Radetsky, P. (1988). *PaceWalking: The balanced way to aerobic health.* New York: Crown.

Kahnert, J. H. (1981). *Excellence in physical fitness* (2d ed.). Dubuque: Kendall/Hunt.

Kashiwa, A., & Rippe, J. (1987). *Fitness walking for women.* New York: Putnam.

Kline, G., Porcari, J., Freedson, P., Ward, A., Ross, J., Wilkie, S., & Rippe, J. (1987). Does aerobic capacity affect the validity of the one-mile walk VO2 max prediction? *Medicine and Science in Sports and Exercise, 19,* 528.

Kline, G., Porcari, J., Hindermeister, R., Freedson, P., McCarron, R., Rippe, J., Ross, J., Ward, A., & Gurry, M. (1986). Prediction of VO2 max from a one-mile track walk. *Medicine and Science in Sports and Exercise, 18,* S35.

Kline, G., Porcari, J. P., Hintermeister, R., Freedson, P. S., Ward, A., McCarron, R. F., Ross, J., & Rippe, J. M. (1987). Prediction of VO2 max from a one-mile track walk. *Medicine and Science in Sports and Exercise, 19,* 253.

Koszuta, L. E. Splash on by. (August/September, 1988). *The Walking Magazine,* 65–70.

Kuntzleman, C. T., & Editors of Consumer Guide. (1978). *The complete book of walking.* New York: Simon and Schuster.

Kusinitz, I., & Fine, M. (1987). *Your guide to getting fit.* Palo Alto, CA: Mayfield.

Lafferty, G., Varnes, J., Paul, T., and Rodovich, F. (1988). *Wellness: Promoting positive lifestyles.* Winston-Salem, NC: Hunter.

Lamb, D. R. (1984). *Physiology of exercise: Responses and adaptations* (2d ed.). New York: Macmillan.

Levy, M. R., Dignan, M., & Shirreffs, J. H. (1988). *Essentials of life and health* (5th ed.). New York: Random House.

McArdle, W. D., Katch, F. I., & Katch, V. L. (1986). *Exercise physiology: Energy, nutrition, and human performance* (2d ed.). Philadelphia: Lea & Febiger.

McCarron, R., Kline, G., Freedson, P., Ward, A., & Rippe, J. (1986). Fast walking is an adequate aerobic stimulus for high fit males. *Medicine and Science in Sports and Exercise, 18,* S21.

McGlynn, G. (1987). *Dynamics of fitness: A practical approach.* Dubuque: Wm. C. Brown.

Makalous, S. L., Arauj, M. A., & Thomas, T. R. (1988). Energy expenditure during walking with hand weights. *The Physician and Sportsmedicine, 16* (4), 139–148.

Mazzeo, K. S. (1985). *A commitment to fitness*. Englewood, CO: Morton.

Melograno, V. J., & Klinzing, J. E. (1988). *An orientation to total fitness* (4th ed.). Dubuque: Kendall/Hunt.

Miller, D. K., & Allen, T. E. (1986). *Fitness: A lifetime commitment* (3d ed.). Edina, MN: Burgess.

Montoye, H. J., Christian, J. L., Nagle, F. J., & Levin, S. M. (1988). *Living fit*. Menol Park, CA: Benjamin/Cummings.

Mullen, K. D., Gold, R. S., Belcastro, P. A. and McDermott, R. J. (1986). *Connections for health*. Dubuque: Wm. C. Brown.

Noble, B. J. (1986). *Physiology of exercise and sport*. St. Louis: Times Mirror/Mosby.

O'Hanley, S., Ward, A., Zwiren, L., McCarron, R., Ross, J., & Rippe, J. M. (1987). Validation of a one-mile walk test in 70–79 year olds. *Medicine and Science in Sports and Exercise, 19*, 528.

Payne, W. A., and Hahn, D. B. 1989. *Understanding your health* (2d ed.). St. Louis: Times/Mirror Mosby.

Porcari, J., Kline, G., Hintermeister, R., Freedson, P., Ward, A., Gurry, M., Ross, J., McCarron, R., & Rippe, J. (1986). Is fast walking an adequate aerobic training stimulus? *Medicine and Science in Sports and Exercise, 18*, S81.

Porcari, J., McCarron, R., Kline, G., Freedson, P., Ward, A., Ross, J., & Rippe, J. (1987). Is fast walking an adequate aerobic training stimulus in 30–69 year old adults? *The Physician and Sports Medicine, 15*, 119.

Prentice, W. E., & Bucher, C. A. (1988). *Fitness for college and life* (2d ed.). St. Louis: Times Mirror/Mosby.

Rippe, J., Ross, J., Gurry, M., Hitzhusen, J., & Freedson, P. (1985). *Cardiovascular effects of walking*. Proceedings of the Second International Conference of Physical Activity, Aging, and Sports, July, p. 47.

Rippe, J., Ross, J., McCarron, R., Porcari, J., Kline, G., Ward, A., Gurry, M., & Freedson, P. (1986). One-mile walk time norms for healthy adults. *Medicine and Science in Sports and Exercise, 18*, S21.

Rippe, J. M., Ward, A., & Freedson, P. (1988). Walking for health and fitness. *Encyclopedia Brittanica Medical and Health Annual*.

Ross, J., Gurry, M., Ward, A., Walcott, G., Hitzhusen, J., & Rippe, J. (1986). Accuracy of predicted max heart rate in the elderly. *Medicine and Science in Sports and Exercise, 18*, S95.

Schwartz, L. (1987). *Heavyhands walking*. Pennsylvania: Rodale.

Seiger, L. H. and Hesson, J. L. (1990). *Walking for Fitness*. Dubuque, IA: Wm. C. Brown.

Stokes, R., & Faris, D. D. (1983). *Fitness everyone*. Winston-Salem, NC: Hunter.

Stokes, R., Moore, A. C., & Moore, C. (1986). *Fitness: The new wave*. (2d ed.). Winston-Salem, NC: Hunter.

Stutman, F. A., & Africano, L. (1985). *The doctor's walking book*. New York: Ballantine.

Sweetgall, R., & Dignam, J. (1986). *The walker's journal*. Delaware: Creative Walking.

Sweetgall, R., Rippe, J., & Katch, F. (1985). *Rockport's fitness walking*. New York: Putnam.

Terry, J. W., Johnson, D. J., & Erickson, C. R. (1984). *Physical activity for all ages: Concepts of high-level wellness* (2d ed.). Dubuque: Kendall/Hunt.

Thaxton, N. A. (1988). *Pathways to fitness: Foundations, motivation, applications*. New York: Harper & Row.

Vitale, F. (1973). *Individualized fitness programs*. Englewood Cliffs, NJ: Prentice-Hall.

Walcott, G., Coleman, R., MacVeigh, M., Ross, J., Gurry, M., Ward, A., Kline, G., & Rippe, J. (1986). Heart rate and VO2 max response to weighted walking. *Medicine and Science in Sports and Exercise, 18*, S28.

Walking for fitness, a round table. (1986). *The Physician and Sportsmedicine, 14*(10), 145–149.

Ward, A., Wilkie, S., O'Hanley, S., Trask, C., Kallmes, D., Kleinerman, J., Crawford, B., Freedson, P., & Rippe, J. (1987). Estimation of VO2 max in overweight females. *Medicine and Science in Sports and Exercise, 19,* 528.

Weinberg, R., Caldwell, P., Cornelius, W., Jackson, A., & Smith, J. (1982). *Health-related fitness: Theory and practice.* Topeka, KS: Jostens.

Wilkie, S., O'Hanley, S., Ward, A., Zwiren, L., Freedson, P., Crawford, B., Kleinerman, J., & Rippe, J. (1987). Estimation of VO2 max from a one-mile walk test using recovery heart rate. *Medicine and Science in Sports and Exercise, 19,* 528.

Williams, M. H. (1985). *Lifetime physical fitness: A personal choice.* Dubuque: Wm. C. Brown.

Williams, S. R. (1988). *Basic nutrition and diet therapy* (2d ed.). St. Louis: Times Mirror/Mosby.

Wilmore, J. H. & Costill, D. L. (1988). *Training for sport and activity: The physiological basis of the conditioning process* (3d ed.). Dubuque: Wm. C. Brown.

Yanker, G. (1983). *The complete book of exercisewalking.* Chicago: Contemporary.

Yanker, G. (1985). *Gary Yanker's walking workouts.* New York: Warner.

Zwiren, L. D., Freedson, P. S., Ward, A., Wilkie, S., & Rippe, J. (1987). Prediction of VO2 max: Comparison of 5 submaximal tests. *Medicine and Science in Sports and Exercise, 19,* 564.

Index